A Year with
Dietrich Bonhoeffer

A Year with
Dietrich Bonhoeffer

Daily Meditations from His Letters,
Writings, and Sermons

Dietrich Bonhoeffer
Edited by Carla Barnhill

HarperOne
An Imprint of HarperCollinsPublishers

HarperOne

A YEAR WITH DIETRICH BONHOEFFER: *Daily Meditations from His Letters, Writings, and Sermons.* Copyright © 2005 by HarperSanFrancisco. All rights reserved. Printed in the United States of America. No part of this book may be used or reproduced in any manner whatsoever without written permission except in the case of brief quotations embodied in critical articles and reviews. For information, address HarperCollins Publishers, 195 Broadway, New York, NY 10007.

HarperCollins books may be purchased for educational, business, or sales promotional use. For information, please e-mail the Special Markets Department at SPsales@harpercollins.com.

HarperCollins Web site: http://www.harpercollins.com

HarperCollins®, 📖 ®, and HarperOne™ are trademarks of HarperCollins Publishers.

Library of Congress Cataloging-in-Publication Data
Bonhoeffer, Dietrich, 1906–1945.
  [Selections. English. 2005]
  A year with Dietrich Bonhoeffer : daily meditations from his letters, writing,s and sermons / Dietrich Bonhoeffer ; edited by Carla Barnhill. — 1st ed.
    p. cm.
ISBN: 978–0–06–088408–6
  . Devotional calendars. I. Barnhill, Carla. II. Title.
BV4811.B584213   2005
242'2—dc22   2005052689

  14 15 RRD(H) 20 19 18 17 16 15 14 13 12 11

When I First Met Bonhoeffer

When I first met Dietrich Bonhoeffer, through reading his books as a young seminarian, he explained the world of faith to me. This young German theologian who was executed by the Nazis for his opposition to Hitler helped me to understand the difficult religious experiences I had known in America.

The evangelical Christian world I had grown up in talked incessantly about Christ but never paid any attention to the things that Jesus taught. Jesus Christ was to be praised but not followed; salvation became an intellectual assent to a concept. "Jesus died for your sins and if you accept that fact you will go to heaven, if you really mean it and pray these words after me." That was the message from the evangelists of my childhood—rather than encouraging any radical turnabout in anyone's life direction (which I later learned was the more biblical notion of conversion). And when it came to the big issues that cropped up for me as a teenager—racism, poverty, and war—I was told explicitly that Christianity had nothing to do with them: they were political, and our faith was personal. On those great social issues, the Christians I knew believed and acted just like everybody else I knew—like white people on racism, like affluent people on poverty, and like patriotic Americans on war.

I had just come back to Jesus after rejecting my childhood faith and joining the student movements of my generation when I discovered for the first time the Sermon on the Mount as the manifesto for a whole new order called the kingdom of God. I discovered Matthew 25: "As you have done to the least of these, you have done to me."

Then I read Bonhoeffer's *Cost of Discipleship*, which relies heavily on the Beatitudes from the Sermon on the Mount and the idea that our treatment of the oppressed is a test of faith. To believe in Jesus means to follow him, said this inspired leader of the Confessing Church, those German Christians who opposed the false religion of Hitler's National Socialism. Their story of radical faithfulness was one from church history that I had never heard. Believing in Jesus is not enough, said Bonhoeffer. We are called to obey his words, to live by what Jesus said, to show our allegiance to the kingdom of God, which had broken into the world through Christ. What a radical idea! Such an obvious one, yet one almost entirely missed by the American churches of the twentieth century. Dietrich Bonhoeffer warned of the "cheap grace" that promotes belief without obedience, and I knew exactly what that meant. He spoke of "costly discipleship" and asked how the grace that came at the tremendous cost of the cross could require so little of us.

We fledgling seminarians in Chicago were catching fire with the idea of "radical discipleship" and Bonhoeffer provided us the textbook and roadmap. "When Christ calls a man, he bids him come and die," said Bonhoeffer. And, all of a sudden, we were faced with a real choice about our lives, not just about our doctrine. "Christianity without the living Christ is inevitably Christianity without discipleship," he said, "and Christianity without discipleship is always Christianity without Christ. It remains an abstract idea, a myth."

I realized that what I had mostly experienced was an American Christianity without Christ, a religion highly conformed to its culture and uncritical of its nation. As Larry Rasmussen summarizes in his book, *Dietrich Bonhoeffer: His Significance for North Americans*: "A Christology that is not simultaneously a social ethic is not a biblical Christology."

At the same time, I had just experienced a secular student movement that had lost its way, had no firm foundations to build upon, and offered no spiritual compass for people's lives or their politics. Without any spiritual or moral depth, protest often turned to bitterness, cynicism, or despair. Finding Jesus again, after years of alienation from the churches, reenergized my young social conscience and provided a basis for both my personal life and my activist vision. Here again Bonhoeffer showed the way, by providing the deep connection between spirituality and moral leadership, religion and public life, faith and politics. Here was a man of prayer who became a man of action—precisely because of his faith.

The more I read Bonhoeffer, the more I was amazed. He seemed to defy all categorization. He was a brilliant intellectual (earning his Ph.D. at the age of twenty-one), yet he felt called by the crisis of his historical moment to act, not just to think. He was profoundly pastoral and was responsible for the training of pastors for the underground seminary of the Confessing Church at Finkenwalde, but taught his students of their responsibility, not just for their parishioners but for the world. He was both a contemplative and an activist (to use those modern terms), who showed, as Thomas Merton later did, that you really can't be one without becoming the other.

Bonhoeffer's insistence on a life of personal discipleship to give belief its credibility was matched by his conviction that a life of community was the essential way that faith would be communicated and demonstrated in the world. You couldn't live the Christian faith alone, he suggested.

All these paradoxes were necessarily complementary for Bonhoeffer, and formed an integrated faith and life rare in his time or any time. Most religious leaders are more one thing than another—theologian or practitioner, contemplative or activist, pastor or prophet, church or political figure, spiritual resource or worldly teacher. I don't know any modern Christian who combines all those vocations and roles better than did Dietrich Bonhoeffer. When he was executed, though still a young man at the age of thirty-nine, Bonhoeffer may have been the most integrated Christian leader ever.

Because of the person Bonhoeffer was, this volume of daily reflections drawn from his writings is a virtual treasure of spiritual wisdom and social conscience, pastoral care and political resistance, personal direction and communal guidance, theological insight and prayerful reflection. One day you learn how to listen deeply to God and to others, another how to confront secular ideologies and national idolatries, another how to read the Bible, another how to make faith come alive in your world.

Bonhoeffer will appeal today to all who are drawn to Jesus Christ because at the heart of everything he believed and did was the centrality of Christ. The liberal habit of diminishing the divinity of Christ or dismissing his incarnation, cross, and resurrection had no appeal for Bonhoeffer. But his orthodoxy has demanding implications for the believer's life in the world. He refused to sentimentalize Jesus, presenting him as the fully human Son of God who brings about a new order of things. Jesus was not set up on some pedestal as an object of belief and worship. Rather, Dietrich Bonhoeffer made Christ both central in the lives of believers and concrete in the life of the world.

It was Bonhoeffer's radical allegiance to Jesus Christ that engendered his criticism of the narrow and false religion of his day. For him, the religious demands of German nationalism gave way to the lordship of Christ. During a stint at Union Seminary in New York City, Bonhoeffer's response to theological liberalism was tepid, but he became inspired by his involvement with the Abyssinian Baptist Church in Harlem. Meeting the black church in America showed the young Bonhoeffer again that the real Christ was critical of the majority culture.

Bonhoeffer will appeal today to all those who are hungry for spirituality. But his was not the soft new age variety that focuses on inner feelings and personal enlightenment. Rather, it was Bonhoeffer's spirituality that made him so politically subversive. And it was always his deepening spiritual journey that animated his struggle for justice. Bonhoeffer's commitment to daily prayer and meditation sustained him and gave him courage for his political resistance. But his was never a private spirituality. Bonhoeffer offers us spirituality for public engagement, in a time that cries out for both. He speaks to the contemporary hunger for spirituality but also the quest for social justice. The connection between the two is what the world is waiting for, and Bonhoeffer is one of the best resources we have for making that critical connection.

Bonhoeffer will appeal today to all those who love the church and long for its renewal. But they won't find in Bonhoeffer somebody who was primarily concerned with new techniques for more contemporary worship, management models for effective church growth, or culturally relevant ways to appeal to the suburban seekers. Bonhoeffer's primary concern for the church was that it be faithful to Christ in the world. He believed that the church itself was meant to be the embodiment of Christ in history, the very demonstration of the meaning of the kingdom of God in society. Bonhoeffer could not imagine the life of solitary discipleship apart from the community of believers. But he would not tolerate the communal life of the church being more conformed to the world than being a prophetic witness to it. For Bonhoeffer, the church was meant to be an alternative community in any society, demonstrating the meaning of Christ in the world and, indeed, providing the principle way the world would learn who Jesus was. He says, "Since the ascension, Christ's place on earth has been taken by his Body, the Church. The Church is the real presence of Christ. . . . The Church is not a religious community of worshippers of Christ but is Christ Himself who has taken form among men. . . . The Church is nothing but a section of humanity in which Christ has really taken form."

Two of the best Bonhoeffer scholars, F. Burton Nelson and Geffrey B. Kelly, in their book, "*The Cost of Moral Leadership: The Spirituality of Dietrich Bonhoeffer*," describe his faith as "Christocentric spirituality" and his view of the church as the conviction that "Christ's presence does indeed transform communities into spiritual centers for God's healing power in the world." It was Dietrich

Bonhoeffer's Christology (view of Christ) and his ecclesiology (view of the church) that would ultimately cost him his life. From his first anti-Hitler sermon in 1933, days after Hitler became chancellor, though his leadership in the Confessing Church and his involvement in the conspiracy that resulted in his execution, Bonhoeffer's political activity was always based in trust in God, obedient discipleship to Jesus Christ, and the guidance of the Holy Spirit, all expressed in Christian community living in compassionate solidarity with the oppressed.

And, of course, Bonhoeffer appeals today to all those who seek to join religion and public life, faith and politics. Because he doesn't fit neatly into the categories of left and right, liberal and conservative, Bonhoeffer can speak to Democrats trying to get religion, to Republicans who want a broader approach than hot-button social issues, and to people who are unhappy with our contemporary political options. Bonhoeffer's deeply personal faith had clear political consequences. He was drawn to the nonviolence of Jesus and, like Martin Luther King Jr., was planning to visit Gandhi in India to learn more about nonviolent resistance. Also like King, he was killed before he could make the trip. But Bonhoeffer's pacifism gave way to what he saw as the overriding need to confront the massive evil of Nazism by participating in a plot to assassinate Adolf Hitler.

Yet, according to Nelson and Kelly, he believed that violence was "still a denial of the gospel teachings of Jesus," and his decision to join the conspiracy against Hitler was accompanied by "ambiguity, sin, and guilt" that were only expiated by a reliance on Christ who "takes on the guilt of sinners, and extends the forgiveness of his Father God to those sinners." That decision, which cost him his life, demonstrates Bonhoeffer's profound wrestling with the always-difficult questions of how faith is to be applied to a world of often imperfect choices.

Bonhoeffer rejected the easier option of political withdrawal that was available to him. He returned to Germany from the United States when many warned him against it, saying, "I will have no right to participate in the reconstruction of Christian life in Germany after the war if I do not share in the trials of this time with my people." Because he chose the path of risk, went to jail, and gave up his life, Dietrich Bonheffer stands alongside Martin Luther King Jr. (both were killed at the age of 39), Salvadoran archbishop Oscar Romero, and many others whose faith led them to make the ultimate sacrifice. Dietrich Bonhoeffer was a Christian martyr whose life and death show us the road to faith. This collection of 365 road signs, one for every day of the year, is a wonderful way to begin again the journey for ourselves.

Jim Wallis
October 2005

January

God's Unfathomable Love

Behold God become human, the unfathomable mystery of the love of God for the world. God loves human beings. God loves the world. Not an ideal human, but human beings as they are; not an ideal world, but the real world. What we find repulsive in their opposition to God, what we shrink back from with pain and hostility, namely, real human beings, the real world, this is for God the ground of unfathomable love. God establishes a most intimate unity with this. God becomes human, a real human being. While we exert ourselves to grow beyond our humanity, to leave the human behind us, God becomes human; and we must recognize that God wills that we be human, real human beings. While we distinguish between pious and godless, good and evil, noble and base, God loves real people without distinction. God has no patience with our dividing the world and humanity according to our standards and imposing ourselves as judges over them. God leads us into absurdity by becoming a real human being and a companion of sinners, thereby forcing us to become the judges of God. God stands beside the real human being and the real world against all their accusers. So God becomes accused along with human beings and the world, and thus the judges become the accused.

—from *Ethics* 84

Noble Humanity

It [is] not enough to say that God embraces human beings. This affirmation rests on an infinitely deeper one, a sentence with a more impenetrable meaning, that God, in the conception and birth of Jesus Christ, has taken on humanity bodily. God overrules every reproach of untruth, doubt, and uncertainty raised against God's love by entering as a human being into human life, by taking on and bearing bodily the nature, essence, guilt, and suffering of human beings. God becomes human out of love for humanity. God does not seek the most perfect human being with whom to be united, but takes on human nature as it is. Jesus Christ is not the transfiguration of noble humanity but the Yes of God to real human beings, not the dispassionate Yes of a judge but [the] merciful Yes of a compassionate sufferer. In this Yes all the life and all the hope of the world are comprised. In the human Jesus Christ the whole of humanity has been judged; again this is not the uninvolved judgment of a judge, but the merciful judgment of one who has borne and suffered the fate of all humanity. Jesus is not *a* human being but *the* human being. What happens to him happens to human beings. It happens to all and therefore to us. The name of Jesus embraces in itself the whole of humanity and the whole of God.

—from *Ethics* 84–85

The Face of Evil

The message of God's becoming human attacks the heart of an era when contempt for humanity or idolization of humanity is the height of all wisdom, among bad people as well as good. The weaknesses of human nature appear more clearly in a storm than in the quiet flow of calmer times. Among the overwhelming majority of people, anxiety, greed, lack of independence, and brutality show themselves to be the mainspring of behavior in the face of unsuspected chance and threats. At such a time the tyrannical despiser of humanity* easily makes use of the meanness of the human heart by nourishing it and giving it other names. Anxiety is called responsibility; greed is called industriousness; lack of independence becomes solidarity; brutality becomes masterfulness. By this ingratiating treatment of human weaknesses, what is base and mean is generated and increased ever anew. The basest contempt for humanity carries on its sinister business under the most holy assertions of love for humanity. The meaner the baseness becomes, the more willing and pliant a tool it is in the hand of the tyrant. The small number of upright people will be smeared with mud. Their courage is called revolt, their discipline Pharisaism, their independence arbitrariness, and their masterfulness arrogance.

—from *Ethics* 85–86

Bonhoeffer is, of course, referring to Adolf Hitler.

The Sin of Contempt

For the tyrannical despiser of humanity, popularity is a sign of the greatest love for humanity. He hides his secret profound distrust of all people behind the stolen words of true community. While he declares himself before the masses to be one of them, he praises himself with repulsive vanity and despises the rights of every individual. He considers the people stupid, and they become stupid; he considers them weak, and they become weak; he considers them criminal, and they become criminal. His most holy seriousness is frivolous play; his conventional protestations of solicitude for people are bare-faced cynicism. In his deep contempt for humanity, the more he seeks the favor of those he despises, the more certainly he arouses the masses to declare him a god. Contempt for humanity and idolization of humanity lie close together. Good people, however, who see through all this, who withdraw in disgust from people and leave them to themselves, and who would rather tend to their own gardens than debase themselves in public life, fall prey to the same temptation to have contempt for humanity as do bad people. Their contempt for humanity is of course more noble, more upright, but at the same time less fruitful, poorer in deeds. Faced by God's becoming human, this contempt will stand the test no better than that of the tyrant. The despiser of humanity despises what God has loved, despises the very form of God become human.

—from *Ethics* 86–87

God's Promises Kept

God does not give us everything we want, but God does fulfill all God's promises, i.e., God remains the Lord of the earth, God preserves the Church, constantly renewing our faith and not laying on us more than we can bear, gladdening us with Divine nearness and help, hearing our prayers, and leading us along the best and straightest paths to holiness. By God's faithfulness in doing this, God creates in us praise for God alone.

—from *Letters and Papers from Prison* 206

The Scope of Life

Again and again it is something of an inward struggle to keep soberly to the facts, to banish illusions and fancies from my head, and to content myself with things as they are; for when one does not understand the external factors, one supposes that there must be some unseen internal factor at work. Besides, our generation cannot now lay claim to such a life as was possible in [our parents' generation]—a life that can find its full scope in professional and personal activities, and achieve balance and fulfillment. That is perhaps the greatest sacrifice that we younger people, with the example of [the previous generation's] life still before our eyes, are called on and compelled to make, and it makes us particularly aware of the fragmentary and incomplete nature of our own. But this very fragmentariness may, in fact, point toward a fulfillment beyond the limits of human achievement; I have to keep that in mind, particularly in view of the death of so many of the best of my former pupils. Even if the pressure of outward events may split our lives into fragments, like bombs falling on houses, we must do our best to keep in view how the whole was planned and thought out; and we shall still be able to see what material was used, or was to be used, here for building.

—from *Letters and Papers from Prison* 59–60

The God of the Wicked

During stable times, when the law reigns and lawbreakers are cast out and ostracized, it is through figures like the tax collector and the prostitute that the gospel of Jesus Christ becomes clear to us. "The tax collectors and the prostitutes may go into the kingdom of heaven ahead of you" (Matt. 21:31). In times that are out of joint, when lawlessness and wickedness arrogantly triumph, the gospel will instead demonstrate itself in the few remaining figures who are just, truthful, and humane. In other times it happened that the wicked found their way to Christ while the good stayed away. Our experience is that the good rediscover Christ while the wicked harden their hearts against him. Other times could preach that unless you have become a sinner like this tax collector and this prostitute, you cannot know and find Christ. We must rather say: unless you have become a righteous person like those who struggle and suffer for justice, truth, and humanity, you cannot know and find Christ. Both sentences are equally paradoxical and impossible as such. But they capture the situation. Christ belongs to the wicked and the good. Christ belongs to both only as sinners, which means as those who, in their wickedness and in their goodness, have fallen away from the origin. Christ calls them back to the origin so that they may be no longer be the wicked and the good, but justified and sanctified sinners.

—from *Ethics* 347–348

God's Image

God does not want me to model others into the image that seems good to me, that is, into my own image. Instead, in their freedom from me God made other people in God's own image. I can never know in advance how God's image should appear in others. That image always takes on a completely new and unique form whose origin is found solely in God's free and sovereign act of creation. To me that form may seem strange, even ungodly. But God creates every person in the image of God's Son, the Crucified, and this image, likewise, certainly looked strange and ungodly to me before I grasped it. Strong and weak, wise or foolish, talented or untalented, pious or less pious, the complete diversity of individuals in the community is no longer a reason to talk and judge and condemn, and therefore no longer a pretext for self-justification. Rather this diversity is a reason for rejoicing in one another and serving one another.

—from *Life Together* 90

A Place for All

Even in this new situation all the members of the community are given their special place; this is no longer the place, however, in which they can most successfully promote themselves, but the place where they can best carry out their service. In a Christian community, everything depends on whether each individual is an indispensable link in a chain. The chain is unbreakable only when even the smallest link holds tightly with the others. A community which permits within itself members who do nothing will be destroyed by them. Thus it is a good idea that all members receive a definite task to perform for the community, so that they may know in times of doubt that they too are not useless and incapable of doing anything. Every Christian community must know that not only do the weak need the strong, but also that the strong cannot exist without the weak. The elimination of the weak is the death of the community.

—from *Life Together* 95–96

Listen

Just as our love for God begins with listening to God's Word, the beginning of love for other Christians is learning to listen to them. God's love for us is shown by the fact that God not only gives us God's Word, but also lends us God's ear. We do God's work for our brothers and sisters when we learn to listen to them. So often Christians, especially preachers, think that their only service is always to have to "offer" something when they are together with other people. They forget that listening can be a greater service than speaking. Many people seek a sympathetic ear and do not find it among Christians, because these Christians are talking even when they should be listening. But Christians who can no longer listen to one another will soon no longer be listening to God either; they will always be talking even in the presence of God. The death of the spiritual life starts here, and in the end there is nothing left but empty spiritual chatter and clerical condescension which chokes on pious words. Those who cannot listen long and patiently will always be talking past others, and finally no longer will even notice it. Those who think their time is too precious to spend listening will never really have time for God and others, but only for themselves and for their own words and plans.

—from *Life Together* 98

The Ears of God

For Christians, pastoral care differs essentially from preaching in that here the task of listening is joined to the task of speaking the Word. There is also a kind of listening with half an ear that presumes already to know what the other person has to say. This impatient, inattentive listening really despises the other Christian and finally is only waiting to get a chance to speak and thus to get rid of the other. This sort of listening is no fulfillment of our task. And it is certain that here, too, in our attitude toward other Christians we simply see reflected our own relationship to God. It should be no surprise that we are no longer able to perform the greatest service of listening that God has entrusted to us—hearing the confession of another Christian—if we refuse to lend our ear to another person on lesser subjects. The pagan world today knows something about persons who often can be helped only by having someone who will seriously listen to them. On this insight it has built its own secular form of pastoral care, which has become popular with many people, including Christians. But Christians have forgotten that the ministry of listening has been entrusted to them by the one who is indeed the great listener and in whose work they are to participate. We should listen with the ears of God, so that we can speak the Word of God.

—from *Life Together* 99

Bear One Another

Christians must bear the burden of one another. They must suffer and endure one another. Only as a burden is the other really a brother or sister and not just an object to be controlled. The burden of human beings was even for God so heavy that God had to go to the cross suffering under it. God truly suffered and endured human beings in the body of Jesus Christ. But in so doing, God bore them as a mother carries her child, as a shepherd the lost lamb. God took on human nature. Then, human beings crushed God to the ground. But God stayed with them and they with God. In suffering and enduring human beings, God maintained community with them. It is the law of Christ that was fulfilled in the cross. Christians share in this law. They are obliged to bear with and suffer one another; but what is more important, now by virtue of the law of Christ having been fulfilled, they are also able to bear one another.

—from *Life Together* 100–101

Freedom of the Other

It is the *freedom* of the other . . . that is a burden to Christians. The freedom of the other goes against Christians' high opinions of themselves, and yet they must recognize it. Christians could rid themselves of this burden by not giving other persons their freedom, thus doing violence to the personhood of others and stamping their own image on others. But when Christians allow God to create God's own image in others, they allow others their own freedom. Thereby Christians themselves bear the burden of the freedom enjoyed by these other creatures of God. All that we mean by human nature, individuality, and talent is part of the other person's freedom—as are the other's weaknesses and peculiarities that so sorely try our patience, and everything that produces the plethora of clashes, differences, and arguments between me and the other. Here, bearing the burden of the other means tolerating the reality of the other's creation by God—affirming it, and in bearing with it, breaking through to delight in it.

—from *Life Together* 101

The Wisdom of Humility

Those who would learn to serve must first learn to think little of themselves. "[You should] not . . . think of yourself more highly that you ought to think" (Rom. 12:3). "The highest and most useful lesson is to truly know yourself and to think humbly of yourself. Making nothing of yourself and always having a good opinion of others is great wisdom and perfection" (Thomas à Kempis). "Do not claim to be wiser than you are" (Rom. 12:17). Only those who live by the forgiveness of their sin in Jesus Christ will think little of themselves in the right way. They will know that their own wisdom completely came to an end when Christ forgave them. They remember the cleverness of the first human beings, who wanted to know what is good and evil and died in this cleverness. The first person, however, who was born on this earth was Cain, the murderer of his brother. His crime is the fruit of humanity's wisdom. Because they can no longer consider themselves wise, Christians will also have a modest opinion of their own plans and intentions. They will know that it is good for their own will to be broken in their encounter with their neighbor. They will be ready to consider their neighbor's will more important and urgent than their own. What does it matter if our own plans are thwarted? Is it not better to serve our neighbors than to get our own way?

—from *Life Together* 96

The Worst of Sinners

One extreme statement must still be made, without any platitudes, and in all soberness. Not considering oneself wise, but associating with the lowly, means considering oneself the worst of sinners. This arouses total opposition not only from those who live at the level of nature, but also from Christians who are self-aware. It sounds like an exaggeration, an untruth. Yet even Paul said of himself that he was the foremost, i.e., the worst of sinners (I Tim. 1:15). He said this at the very place in Scripture where he was speaking of his ministry as an apostle. There can be no genuine knowledge of sin that does not lead me down to this depth. If my sin appears to me to be in any way smaller or less reprehensible in comparison with the sins of others, then I am not yet recognizing my sin at all. My sin is of necessity the worst, the most serious, the most objectionable. Christian love will find any number of excuses for the sins of others; only for my sin is there no excuse whatsoever. That is why my sin is the worst. Those who would serve others in the community must descend all the way down to this depth of humility. How could I possibly serve other persons in unfeigned humility if their sins appear to me to be seriously worse than my own? If I am to have any hope for them, then I must not raise myself above them. Such service would be a sham.

—from *Life Together* 97–98

Weakness and Wickedness

It is in just such times that we should make an effort to remember in our prayers how much we have to be thankful for. Above all, we should never allow ourselves to be consumed by the present moment, but should foster that calmness that comes from noble thoughts, and measure everything by them. The fact that most people cannot do this is what makes it so difficult to bear with them. It is weakness rather than wickedness that perverts people and drags us down, and it needs profound sympathy to put up with that. But all the time God still reigns in heaven.

—from *Letters and Papers from Prison* 204–205

A Letter to Maria

When I also think about the situation of the world, the complete darkness over our personal fate and my present imprisonment, then I believe that our union can only be a sign of God's grace and kindness, which calls us to faith. We would be blind if we did not see it. Jeremiah says at the moment of his people's great need "still one shall buy houses and acres in this land" as a sign of trust in the future. This is where faith belongs. May God give it to us daily. And I do not mean the faith which flees the world, but the one that endures the world and which loves and remains true to the world in spite of all the suffering which it contains for us. Our marriage shall be a yes to God's earth; it shall strengthen our courage to act and accomplish something on the earth. I fear that Christians who stand with only one leg upon earth also stand with only one leg in heaven.

—from *A Testament to Freedom* 488

On January 17, 1943, Bonhoeffer becomes engaged to Maria van Wedemeyer.

Farewell Maria

These will be quiet days in our homes. But I have had the experience over and over again that the quieter it is around me, the clearer do I feel the connection to you. It is as though in solitude the soul develops senses which we hardly know in everyday life. Therefore I have not felt lonely or abandoned for one moment. You, the parents, all of you, the friends and students of mine at the front, all are constantly present to me. Your prayers and good thoughts, words from the Bible, discussions long past, pieces of music, and books—[all these] gain life and reality as never before. It is a great invisible sphere in which one lives and in whose reality there is no doubt. If it says in the old children's song about the angels: "Two, to cover me, two, to wake me," so is this guardianship, by good invisible powers in the morning and at night, something which grownups need today no less than children. Therefore you must not think that I am unhappy. What is happiness and unhappiness? It depends so little on the circumstances; it depends really only on that which happens inside a person. I am grateful every day that I have you, and that makes me happy.

—from *A Testament to Freedom* 490

The Nature of Church

The space of the church is the place where witness is given to the foundation of all reality in Jesus Christ. The church is the place where it is proclaimed and taken seriously that God has reconciled the world to himself in Christ, that God so loved the world that God gave his Son for it. The space of the church is not there in order to fight with the world for a piece of its territory, but precisely to testify to the world that it is still the world, namely, the world that is loved and reconciled by God. It is not true that the church intends to or must spread its space out over the space of the world. It desires no more space than it needs to serve the world with its witness to Jesus Christ and to the world's reconciliation to God through Jesus Christ. The church can only defend its own space by fighting, not for space, but for the salvation of the world. Otherwise the church becomes a "religious society" that fights in its own interest and thus has ceased to be the church of God in the world. So the first task given to those who belong to the church of God is not to be something for themselves, for example, by creating a religious organization or leading a pious life, but to be witnesses of Jesus Christ to the world.

—from *Ethics* 63–64

Seeking Goodness

Those who wish even to focus on the problem of a Christian ethic are faced with an outrageous demand—from the outset they must give up, as inappropriate to this topic, the very two questions that led them to deal with the ethical problem: "How can I be good?" and "How can I do something good?" Instead they must ask the wholly other, completely different question: what is the will of God? This demand is radical precisely because it presupposes a decision about ultimate reality, that is, a decision of faith. When the ethical problem presents itself essentially as the question of my own being good and doing good, the decision has already been made that the self and the world are the ultimate realities. All ethical reflection then has the goal that I be good, and that the world—by my action—becomes good. If it turns out, however, that these realities, myself and the world, are themselves embedded in a wholly other ultimate reality, namely, the reality of God the Creator, Reconciler, and Redeemer, then the ethical problem takes on a whole new aspect. Of ultimate importance, then, is not that I become good, or that the condition of the world be improved by my efforts, but that the reality of God show itself everywhere to be the ultimate reality.

—from *Ethics* 47–48

The Distorted Mirror

Where God is known by faith to be the ultimate reality, the source of my ethical concern will be that God be known as the good, even at the risk that I and the world are revealed as not good, but as bad through and through. All things appear as in a distorted mirror if they are not seen and recognized in God. All that is—so to speak—given, all laws and norms, are abstractions, as long as God is not known in faith to be the ultimate reality. That God alone is the ultimate reality, is, however, not an idea meant to sublimate the actual world, nor is it the religious perfecting of a profane worldview. It is rather a faithful Yes to God's self-witness, God's revelation. . . . But then the decision about the whole of life depends on our relation to God's revelation. Awareness of it is not only a step-by-step progress in the discovery of deeper and more inward realities, but this awareness is the turning point, the pivot, of all perception of reality as such. The ultimate, or final, reality discloses itself to be at the same time the first reality, God as the first and the last, the Alpha and Omega. Without God, all seeing and perceiving of things and laws become abstraction, a separation from both origin and goal.

—from *Ethics* 48–49

The Good Fruit

There is an old argument about whether only the will, the act of the mind, the person, can be good, or whether achievement, work, consequence, or condition can be called good as well—and if so, which comes first and which is more important. This argument, which has also seeped into theology, leading there as elsewhere to serious aberrations, proceeds from a basically perverse way of putting the question. It tears apart what is originally and essentially one, namely, the good and the real, the person and the work. The objection that Jesus, too, had this distinction between person and work in mind, when he spoke about the good tree that brings forth good fruits, distorts this saying of Jesus into its exact opposite. Its meaning is not that first the person is good and then the work, but that *only the two together*, only both as united in one, are to be understood as good or bad.

—from *Ethics* 51

Real Goodness

The question of good must not be narrowed to investigating the relation of actions to their motives, or to their consequences, measuring them by a ready-made ethical standard. An ethic of disposition or intention is just as superficial as an ethic of consequences. For what right do we have to stay with inner motivation as the ultimate phenomenon of ethics, ignoring that "good" intentions can grow out of very dark backgrounds in human consciousness and subconsciousness, and that often the worst things happen as a result of "good intentions"? As the question of the motives of action finally disappears in the tangled web of the past, so the question of its consequences gets lost in the mists of the future. There are no clear boundaries on either side. Nothing justifies us in stopping at any arbitrary point we choose in order to make a definitive judgment. In practice, we ever and again stop to make such an arbitrary determination, whether along the lines of an ethic of motives or an ethic of consequences. . . . Neither has any fundamental advantage over the other, because in both cases the question of good is posed abstractly, severed from reality. . . . Good is reality, reality itself seen and recognized in God. Human beings, with their motives and their works, with their fellow human beings, with the creation that surrounds them, in other words, reality as a whole held in the hands of God—that is what is embraced by the question of good.

—from *Ethics* 52–53

Answered Prayers

Prayer means nothing else but the readiness to appropriate the Word, and what is more, to let it speak to me in my personal situation, in my particular tasks, decisions, sins, and temptations. What can never enter the prayer of the community may here silently be made known to God. On the basis of the words of Scripture we pray that God may throw light on our day, preserve us from sin, and enable us to grow in holiness, and that we may be faithful in our work and have the strength to do it. And we may be certain that our prayer will be heard because it issues from God's Word and promise. Because God's Word has found its fulfillment in Jesus Christ, all the prayers we pray on the basis of this Word are certainly fulfilled and answered in Jesus Christ.

—from *Life Together* 89

Prayer That Overcomes

All Christians have their own circle of those who have requested them to intercede on their behalf, or people for whom for various reasons they know they have been called upon to pray. First of all, this circle will include those with whom they must live every day. With this we have advanced to the point at which we hear the heartbeat of all Christian life together. A Christian community either lives by the intercessory prayers of its members for one another or the community will be destroyed. I can no longer condemn or hate other Christians for whom I pray, no matter how much trouble they cause me. In intercessory prayer the face that may have been strange and intolerable to me is transformed into the face of one for whom Christ died, the face of a pardoned sinner. That is a blessed discovery for the Christian who is beginning to offer intercessory prayer for others. As far as we are concerned, there is no dislike, no personal tension, no disunity or strife, that cannot be overcome by intercessory prayer. Intercessory prayer is the purifying bath into which the individual and the community must enter every day.

—from *Life Together* 90

God's Love for Our Enemies

Don't believe that you know on your own how to get along with people, or how to deal with enemies, or what good and evil are, lest humankind devour itself completely. "Never be conceited"— rather look to God's way with us, with our enemies, that way, which Scripture itself calls foolish, the way of God's love for our enemies, which God demonstrates to us by sending God's Son all the way to the cross. The best wisdom is recognizing the cross of Jesus Christ as the insuperable love of God for all people, for us as well as for our enemies. Or are we of the opinion that God loves us more than God loves our enemies: Would we believe that we are God's favorite children? Were we to think that, we would show ourselves to be of like mind with the Pharisees; we would have stopped being Christians. Is God's love any less for our enemies, for whom God just as much came, suffered, and died, as God did for us? The cross is nobody's private property, but belongs to all; it is intended for all humanity.

—from *A Testament to Freedom* 285

Resist Conceit

God loves our enemies—the cross tells us that. God suffers on their account, feels anguish and sorrow because of them. God gave the beloved Son for them. That is the whole point every time we encounter enemies we remember at once: God loves them, God gave everything for them. Therefore, never be conceited. With respect to our attitude toward our enemies, this means first, remember that you were God's enemy and that, without having earned it or being worthy of it, you were met with mercy. It means second, remember that God hung on the cross for your enemy too, and love God as God loves you.

—from *A Testament to Freedom* 285–286

Met with Mercy

There are neighbors or others who continually say evil things about us, who abuse us, who openly wrong us, who torment and harass us whenever they can. At the mere sight of them, the blood rushes to our heads, a terrible threatening anger. It is the enemy who provokes such a thing in us. But now we must be on guard. Now we must remember quickly: I was met with mercy, not by people, no, but by God, and Jesus Christ died for our enemy—and all at once everything is different. Now we hear: repay no one evil for evil. Do not lift us your hand to strike, do not open your mouth in anger, but be still. For what can those who do you evil do to harm you? It is not you whom it harms, but it does harm them. No Christian is harmed by suffering injustice. But perpetuating injustice does harm. Indeed, the evil one wants to accomplish only one thing with you; namely, that you also become evil. But were that to happen, the evil one would have won. Therefore, repay no one evil for evil. For in so doing, you harm not the evil one but yourself.

—from *A Testament to Freedom* 286

Live in Peace

Do what is right not only to respectable citizens, but especially to the disrespectable ones as well; be at peace not only with those who are peaceable, but especially with those who do not wish to let us live in peace. Even the heathen can live at peace with those who are peaceable to them. But Jesus Christ died not for those who are respectable and peaceable, but for sinners and enemies, for the disrespectful, for the haters and killers. Our hearts make sure that we only keep the company of friends, of the righteous and the respectable. But Jesus was to be found right in the midst of his enemies. That is precisely where he wanted to be. We should be there too. It is that which distinguishes us from all other teachings and religions. In them, the pious want to be with one another. But Christ wants us to be in the midst of our enemies, as he was; it was in the midst of his enemies that he dies the death of God's love and prayed: Father, forgive them for they know not what they do. Christ wants to win his victory among his enemies. Therefore, do not withdraw, do not seclude yourselves; rather seek to do good unto all. Make peace, as far as it depends on you, with all.

—from *A Testament to Freedom* 286

Evil in Disguise

The great masquerade of evil has played havoc with all our ethical concepts. For evil to appear disguised as light, charity, historical necessity, or social justice is quite bewildering to anyone brought up on our traditional ethical concepts, while for Christians who base their lives on the Bible it merely confirms the fundamental wickedness of evil. . . . Who stands fast? Only those whose final standards are not their reason, their principles, their conscience, their freedom, or their virtue, but who are ready to sacrifice all this when they are called to obedient and responsible action in faith and in exclusive allegiance to God—the responsible ones, who try to make their whole life an answer to the question and call of God.

—from *Letters and Papers from Prison* 2, 4

On January 30, 1933, Adolf Hitler is made chancellor of Germany.

Fooled by Success

Although it is certainly not true that success justifies an evil deed and shady means, it is impossible to regard success as something that is ethically quite neutral. The fact is that historical success creates a basis for the continuance of life, and it is still a moot point whether it is ethically more responsible to take the field like a Don Quixote against a new age, or to admit one's defeat, accept the new age, and agree to serve it. In the last resort success makes history; and the ruler of history repeatedly brings good out of evil over the heads of the history makers. Simply to ignore the ethical significance of success is a short circuit created by dogmatists who think unhistorically and irresponsibly; and it is good for us sometimes to be compelled to grapple seriously with the ethical problem of success. As long as goodness is successful, we can afford the luxury of regarding it as having no ethical significance; it is when success is achieved by evil means that the problem arises. . . . To talk of going down fighting like heroes in the face of certain defeat is not really heroic at all, but merely a refusal to face the future. The ultimate question for responsible people to ask is not how we are to extricate ourselves heroically from the affair, but how the coming generation is to live. It is only from this question, with its responsibility toward history, that fruitful solutions can come, even if for the time being they are very humiliating.

—from *Letters and Papers from Prison* 5–6

February

Facing the Storm

And the more they storm, the more shall we call. And the more we call, the more wildly they storm because where the Word of Christ is truly said, there the world feels that it is either a destructive madness or rather a destructive truth, which is a matter then of life and death. Where truly peace has been spoken, there the war must doubly rage, since it perceives that it is to be finished off. Christ wishes to be its death. But the more passionately and the more faithfully will the church of Christ stand with its Lord and preach his Word of peace, even if it goes through abuse and persecution. . . . War, sickness, and hunger must come so that the gospel of the kingdom of peace, of love and salvation may be said and heard so much more clearly and deeply. The evil powers must serve the gospel; the powers of enmity and of the nations' opposition must also serve, to bring the gospel to all nations, so that it may be heard by all; all these must serve the kingdom which shall belong to all humankind. War serves peace, hate serves love, the devil serves God, the cross serves life. And then, when that becomes manifest, then the end will come; then the Lord of the church will lay his hand of blessing and protection on them, as on his faithful servant.

—from *A Testament to Freedom* 203–204

Absent Justice

It is an evil time when the world lets injustice happen silently, when the oppression of the poor and the wretched cries out to heaven in a loud voice and the judges and rulers of the earth keep silent about it, when the persecuted church calls to God for help in the hour of dire distress and exhorts people to do justice, and yet no mouth on earth is opened to bring justice. "Do you indeed speak righteousness, O you judges, do you judge the children of our people? It is precisely the humankind on whom injustice is perpetuated. Must that always be forgotten in such times? Do you hear it? Children of humankind who are creatures of God like you, who feel pain and misery like you, you who do violence to them; who have their happiness and hopes like you; who feel their honor and their shame like you; your bothers and sisters! Are you mute?" Oh no, they are not mute, their voice is heard on earth. But it is an unmerciful, a partisan word they speak. It judges not by what is right, but by a person's standing.

—from *A Testament to Freedom* 279

On February 2, 1945, death sentences are pronounced on Bonhoeffer's brother and brother-in-law.

The Hands of Injustice

When the mouths of the world's rulers remain silent about injustice, their hands invariably commit acts of violence. This language of human hands where no justice exists is terrible. It is there that the distress and pain of the body originates. It is there that the persecuted, captive, beaten church longs for deliverance from this body. Let me fall into God's hands, but not into the hands of others! Do we still hear it? Christ is speaking here! He experienced the unrighteous judgment, he fell into the hands of men. Innocence is accusing the unrighteous world.

—from *A Testament to Freedom* 279

Belonging to Christ

"Blessed are those who are persecuted for righteousness' sake, for theirs is the kingdom of heaven" (Matt. 5:10). This verse does not speak about the righteousness of God, that is, about persecution for the sake of Jesus Christ; rather, it calls those blessed who are persecuted for a just cause—and, we may now add, for a cause that is true, good, humane (cf. 1 Pet. 3:14 and 2:20). With this beatitude Jesus thoroughly rejects the false timidity of those Christians who evade any kind of suffering for a just, good, and true cause because they supposedly could have a clear conscience only if they were to suffer for the explicit confession of faith in Christ. . . . Jesus cares for those who suffer for a just cause even if it is not exactly for the confession of his name; he brings them under his protection, takes responsibility for them, and addresses them with his claim. Thus the person persecuted for a just cause is led to Christ. Thus it happens that such people, in the hour of their suffering and responsibility—perhaps for the first time in their lives, in a way that is strange and surprising to themselves, but nevertheless as a most deeply felt necessity—call upon Christ and confess themselves to be Christian, because it is only at that moment that an awareness of belonging to Christ dawns on them.

—from *Ethics* 346–347

On February 4, 1906, Dietrich Bonhoeffer is born in Breslau, Germany.

Bread for All Time

Almost all of us have grown up with the idea that the Scripture reading is solely a matter of hearing the Word of God for today. That is why for many the Scripture reading consists only of a few brief selected verses that are to form the central idea of the day. There can be no doubt that the daily Bible passages published by the Moravian Brethren, for example, are a real blessing to all who have ever used them. Many people have realized that to their great amazement and have been grateful for the daily Bible readings particularly during the time of the church struggle. But equally there can be little doubt that brief passages cannot and must not take the place of reading the Scripture as a whole. The verse for the day is not yet the Holy Scriptures that will remain throughout all time until the Day of Judgment. The Holy Scriptures are more than selected Bible passages. It is also more than "Bread for Today." It is God's revealed Word for all peoples, for all times. The Holy Scriptures do not consist of individual sayings, but are a whole and can be used most effectively as such. . . . The full witness to Jesus Christ the Lord can be clearly heard only in its immeasurable inner relationships, in the connection of Old and New Testaments, of promise and fulfillment, sacrifice and law, Law and Gospel, cross and resurrection, faith and obedience, having and hoping.

—from *Life Together* 58–60

The Story of Christ

For those who want to hear, reading the biblical books in a sequential order forces them to go, and to allow themselves to be found, where God has acted once and for all for the salvation of human beings. The historical books of the Holy Scriptures come alive for us in a whole new way precisely when they are read during worship services. We receive a part of that which once took place for our salvation. Forgetting and losing ourselves, we too pass through the Red Sea, through the desert, across the Jordan into the promised land. With Israel we fall into doubt and unbelief and through punishment and repentance experience again God's help and faithfulness. All this is not mere reverie, but holy, divine reality. We are uprooted from our own existence and are taken back to the holy history of God on earth. There God has dealt with us, and there God still deals with us today, with our needs and our sins, by means of the divine wrath and grace. What is important is not that God is a spectator and participant in our life today, but that we are attentive listeners and participants in God's action in the sacred story, the story of Christ on earth.

—from *Life Together* 62

Finding Ourselves in Christ

It is not that God's help and presence must still be proved in our life; rather God's presence and help have been demonstrated for us in the life of Jesus Christ. It is in fact more important for us to know what God did to Israel, in God's son Jesus Christ, than to discover what God intends for us today. The fact that Jesus Christ died is more important than the fact that I will die. And the fact that Jesus Christ was raised from the dead is the sole ground of my hope that I, too, will be raised on the day of judgment. Our salvation is "from outside ourselves." I find salvation not in my life story, but only in the story of Jesus Christ. Only those who allow themselves to be found in Jesus Christ—in the incarnation, cross, and resurrection—are with God and God with them.

—from *Life Together* 62

On February 7, 1945, Bonhoeffer is moved to Buchenwald concentration camp.

Finding God in the Bible

It may be taken as a rule for the correct reading of Scripture that the readers should never identify themselves with the person who is speaking in the Bible. It is not I who am angry, but God; it is not I giving comfort, but God; it is not I admonishing, but God admonishing in the Scriptures. Of course, I will be able to express the fact that it is God who is angry, God who is giving comfort and admonishing, by speaking not in a detached, monotonous voice, but only with heartfelt involvement, as one who knows that I myself am being addressed. However, it will make all the difference between a right and a wrong way of reading Scripture if I do not confuse myself with, but rather quite simply serve, God.

—from *Life Together* 64

A Letter from a Friend

The situation of the one who is reading the Scripture would probably come closest to that in which I read to another person a letter from a friend. I would not read the letter as though I had written it myself. The distance between us would be clearly noticeable as it was read. And yet I would also not be able to read my friend's letter as if it were of no concern to me. On the contrary, because of our close relationship, I would read it with personal interest. Proper reading of Scripture is not a technical exercise that can be learned; it is something that grows or diminishes according to my own spiritual condition. The ponderous, laborious reading of the Bible by many a Christian who has become seasoned through experience often far surpasses a minister's reading, no matter how perfect the latter in form.

—from *Life Together* 64

Co-creative Humanity

We encounter the mandate of work in the Bible already with the first human being. Adam was placed in the garden of Eden "to till it and keep it" (Gen. 2:15). After the fall, work remains a mandate of divine discipline and grace (Gen. 3:17–19). By the sweat of his brow Adam wrests nourishment from the field, and soon the range of human work embraces everything from agriculture through economic activity to science and art (Gen. 4:17ff). The work founded in paradise calls for co-creative human deeds. Through them a world of things and values is created that is destined for the glory and service of Jesus Christ. It is not creation out of nothing, like God's creating, but it is the creation of new things on the basis of God's initial creation. No one can withdraw from this mandate.

—from *Ethics* 70–71

Work in the World

In the work that humans do according to divine commission, a reflection of the heavenly world emerges that reminds those who know Jesus Christ of that world. Cain's first creation was a city, the earthly reflection of the eternal city of God. Then followed the invention of violins and flutes, which give us on earth a foretaste of heavenly music. Then comes the extraction and processing of metallic treasures dug out of the earth, partly to decorate the earthly house like the heavenly city that shines with gold and precious stones, and partly to make swords of avenging justice. Through the divine mandate of work, a world should emerge that—knowingly or unknowingly—expects Christ, is directed toward Christ, is open for Christ, and serves and glorifies Christ.

—from *Ethics* 71

The Welcome of Christ

"Now concerning love of the brothers and sisters, you do not need to have anyone write to you, for you yourselves have been taught by God to love one another. . . . But we urge you, beloved, to do so more and more" (1 Thess. 4:9f). It is God's own undertaking to teach such love. All that human beings can add is to remember this divine instruction and the exhortation to excel in it more and more. When God had mercy on us, when God revealed Jesus Christ to us as our brother, when God won our hearts by God's own love, our instruction in Christian love began at the same time. When God was merciful to us, we learned to be merciful with one another. When we received forgiveness instead of judgment, we too were made ready to forgive each other. What God did to us, we then owed to others. The more we received, the more we were able to give; and the more meager our love for one another, the less we were living by God's mercy and love. Thus God taught us to encounter one another as God encountered us in Christ. "Welcome one another, therefore, just as Christ has welcomed you, for the glory of God" (Rom. 15:7).

—from *Life Together* 33–34

Absent Love

Nothing can make up for the absence of someone whom we love, and it would be wrong to try to find a substitute; we must simply hold out and see it through. That sounds very hard at first, but at the same time it is a great consolation, for the gap, as long as it remains unfilled, preserves the bonds between us. It is nonsense to say that God fills the gap; God does not fill it, but on the contrary, God keeps it empty and so helps us keep alive our former communion with each other, even at the cost of pain. . . . The dearer and richer our memories, the more difficult the separation. But gratitude changes the pangs of memory into a tranquil joy. The beauties of the past are borne, not as a thorn in the flesh, but as a precious gift in themselves. We must take care not to wallow in our memories or to hand ourselves over to them, just as we do not gaze all the time at a valuable present, but only at special times, and apart from these keep it simply as a hidden treasure that is ours for certain. In this way the past gives us lasting joy and strength.

—from *Letters and Papers from Prison* 100–101

Love Song

God wants us to love God eternally with our whole hearts—not in such a way as to injure or weaken our earthly love, but to provide a kind of *cantus firmus* to which the other melodies of life provide the counterpoint. One of these contrapuntal themes (which have their own complete independence but are yet related to the *cantus firmus*) is earthly affection. Even in the Bible we have the Song of Songs; and really one can imagine no more ardent, passionate, sensual love than is portrayed there. It is a good thing that that book is in the Bible, in face of all those who believe that the restraint of passion is Christian (where is there such restraint in the Old Testament?). Where the *cantus firmus* is clear and plain, the counterpoint can be developed to its limits. The two are "undivided and yet distinct," in the words of the Chalcedonian Definition, like Christ in his divine and human natures. . . . Do you see what I am driving at? I wanted to tell you to have a good, clear *cantus firmus;* that is the only way to a full and perfect sound, when the counterpoint has a firm support and cannot come adrift or get out of tune, while remaining a distinct whole in its own right. Only a polyphony of this kind can give life a wholeness and at the same time assure us that nothing calamitous can happen as long as the *cantus firmus* is kept going.

—from *Letters and Papers from Prison* 150–151

The Family of Christ

One is a brother or sister to another only through Jesus Christ. I am a brother or sister to another person through what Jesus Christ has done for me and to me; others have become brothers and sisters to me through what Jesus Christ has done for them and to them. The fact that we are brothers and sisters only through Jesus Christ is of immeasurable significance. Therefore, the other who comes face to face with me earnestly and devoutly seeking community is not the brother or sister with whom I am to relate in the community. My brother or sister is instead that other person who has been redeemed by Christ, absolved from sin, and called to faith and eternal life. What persons are in themselves as Christians, in their inwardness and piety, cannot constitute the basis of our community, which is determined by what those persons are in terms of Christ. Our community consists solely in what Christ has done to both of us. That not only is true at the beginning, as if in the course of time something else were to be added to our community, but also remains so for all the future and into all eternity. . . . The more genuine and the deeper our community becomes, the more everything else between us will recede, and the more clearly and purely will Jesus Christ and his work become the one and only thing that is alive between us. We have one another only through Christ, but through Christ we really do *have* one another. We have one another completely and for all eternity.

—from *Life Together* 34

Daily Attention

Daily, quiet attention to the Word of God which is meant for me, even if it is only for a few minutes, will become for me the focal point of everything which brings inward and outward order into my life. In the interruption and fragmentation of our previous ordered life which this time brings with it, in the danger of losing inner discipline through the host of events, the incessant claims of work and service, through doubt and temptation, struggle and disquiet of all kinds, meditation gives our life something like constancy, it keeps the link with our previous life, from baptism to confirmation, to ordination. It keeps us in the saving fellowship of the community, the brethren, our spiritual home. It is a spark from that hearth which the communities want to keep at home for you. It is a source of peace, of patience, and of joy; it is like a magnet which attracts all the resources of discipline to its poles; it is like a pure, deep water in which the heaven, with its clouds and its sun, is clearly reflected; but it also serves the Highest in showing us a place of discipline and of quietness, of saving order and peace. Have we not all a desire for such a gift, unacknowledged perhaps, but still profound? Could it not again be a healing power for us, leading to recovery?

—*A Testament to Freedom* 457

The Living Jesus

Discipleship is commitment to Christ. Because Christ exists, he must be followed. An idea about Christ, a doctrinal system, a general religious recognition of grace or forgiveness of sins does not require discipleship. In truth, it even excludes discipleship; it is inimical to it. One enters into a relationship with an idea by way of knowledge, enthusiasm, perhaps even by carrying it out, but never by personal obedient discipleship. Christianity without the living Jesus Christ remains necessarily a Christianity without discipleship; and a Christianity without discipleship is always a Christianity without Jesus Christ. It is an idea, a myth. A Christianity in which there is only God the Father, but not Christ as a living Son actually cancels discipleship. In that case there will be trust in God, but not discipleship.

—from *Discipleship* 59

First Response

Following Christ means taking certain steps. The first step, which responds to the call, separates the followers from their previous existence. A call to discipleship thus immediately creates a new situation. Staying in the old situation and following Christ mutually exclude each other. At first, that was quite visibly the case. The tax collector had to leave his booth and Peter his nets to follow Jesus. According to our understanding, even back then things could have been quite different. Jesus could have given the tax collector new knowledge of God and left him in his old situation. If Jesus had not been God's Son become human, then that would have been possible. But because Jesus is the Christ, it has to be made clear from the beginning that his word is not a doctrine. Instead, it creates existence anew. The point was to really walk with Jesus. It was made clear to those he called that they only had one possibility of believing in Jesus, that of leaving everything and going with the incarnate Son of God.

—from *Discipleship* 61–62

Obedience and Belief

There is a great danger in telling the difference between a situation where faith is possible and where it is not. It is clear that there is nothing in the situation as such to indicate which kind it is. Only the call of Jesus Christ qualifies it as a situation where faith is possible. Second, a situation where faith is possible is never made by humans. Discipleship is not a human offer. The call alone creates the situation. Third, the value of the situation is never in itself. The call alone justifies it. Finally and most of all, the situation which enables faith can itself happen only in faith. The concept of a situation in which faith is possible is only a description of the reality contained in the following two statements, both of which are equally true: *only the believers obey,* and *only the obedient believe.*

—from *Discipleship* 63

Grace and Faith

If we ourselves understand our first step as a precondition for grace, for faith, then we are judged by our works and completely cut off from grace.... It is but a new possibility for living within our old existence and thereby a complete misunderstanding. We remain in unbelief. But the external works have to take place; we have to get into the situation of being able to believe. We have to take the step. What does that mean? It means that we take this step in the right way only when we do not look to the necessity of our works, but solely with a view to the word of Jesus Christ, which calls us to take the step. Peter knows that he cannot climb out of the boat by his own power. His first step would already be his downfall, so he calls, "Command me to come to you on the water." Christ answers, "Come." Christ has to have called; the step can be taken only at his word. This call is his grace, which calls us out of death into the new life of obedience.... So it is, indeed, the case that the first step of obedience is itself an act of faith in Christ's word.

—from *Discipleship* 65–66

Disobedient Belief

No one should be surprised that they cannot come to believe so long as, in deliberate disobedience, they flee or reject some aspect of Jesus's commandment. You do not want to subject some sinful passion, an enmity, a hope, your life plans, or your reason to Jesus's commandment? Do not be surprised that you do not receive the Holy Spirit, that you cannot pray, that your prayer for faith remains empty! Instead, go and be reconciled with your sister or brother; let go of the sin which keeps you captive; and you will be able to believe again! If you reject God's commanding word, you will not receive God's gracious word. How would you expect to find community while you intentionally withdraw from it at some point? The disobedient cannot believe; only the obedient believe.

—from *Discipleship* 66

Stepping into Faith

Jesus says to anyone who uses their faith or lack of faith to excuse their acts of disobedience to his call: First obey, do the external works, let go of what binds you, give up what is separating you from God's will! Do not say, I do not have the faith for that. You will not have it so long as you remain disobedient, so long as you will not take that first step. Do not say, I have faith, so I do not have to take the first step. You do not have faith, because and so long as you will not take that first step. Instead, you have hardened yourself in disbelief under the appearance of humble faith. It is an evil excuse to point from inadequate obedience to inadequate faith, and from inadequate faith to inadequate obedience. It is the disobedience of the "faithful" if they confess their unbelief where their obedience is required and if they play games with that confession (Mark 9:24). You believe—so take the first step! It leads to Jesus Christ. You do not believe—take the same step; it is commanded of you! The question of your belief or unbelief is not yours to ask. The works of obedience are required and must be done immediately. The situation is given in which faith becomes possible and really exists.

—from *Discipleship* 66–67

Simple Obedience

Fundamentally eliminating simple obedience introduces a principle of Scripture foreign to the gospel. According to it, in order to understand Scripture, one first must have a key to interpreting it. But that key would not be the living Christ himself in judgment and grace, and using the key would not be according to the will of the living Holy Spirit alone. Rather, the key to Scripture would be a general doctrine of grace, and we ourselves would decide its use. The problem of following Christ shows itself here to be a hermeneutical problem. But it should be clear to a gospel-oriented hermeneutic that we cannot simply identify ourselves directly with those called by Jesus. Instead, those who are called in Scripture themselves belong to the word of God and thus to the proclamation of the word. . . . Simple obedience would be misunderstood hermeneutically if we were to act and follow as if we were contemporaries of the biblical disciples. But the Christ proclaimed to us in Scripture is, through every word he says, the one whose gift of faith is granted only to the obedient, faith to the obedient alone. We cannot and may not go behind the word of Scripture to the actual events. Instead, we are called to follow Christ by the entire word of Scripture, simply because we do not intend to wish to violate Scripture by legalistically applying a principle to it, even that of a doctrine of faith.

—from *Discipleship* 82

Legitimate Obedience

Obedience to Jesus's call is never an autonomous human deed. Thus, not even something like actually giving away one's wealth is the obedience required. It could be that such a step would not be obedience to Jesus at all, but instead, a free choice of one's own lifestyle. It could be a Christian ideal, a Franciscan ideal of poverty. It could be that by giving away wealth, people affirm themselves and an ideal, and not Jesus's command. It could be that they do not become free from themselves, but even more trapped in themselves. The step into the situation is not something people offer Jesus; it is always Jesus's gracious offer to people. It is legitimate only when it is done that way, but then it is no longer a free human possibility.

—from *Discipleship* 83

Prayer and Work

Praying and working are two different things. Prayer should not be hindered by work, but neither should work be hindered by prayer. Just as it was God's will that human beings should work six days and rest and celebrate before the face of God on the seventh, so it is also God's will that every day should be marked for the Christian both by prayer and work. Prayer also requires its own time. But the longest part of the day belongs to work. The inseparable unity of both will only become clear when work and prayer each receives its own undivided due. Without the burden and labor of the day, prayer is not prayer; and without prayer, work is not work. Only the Christian knows that. Thus it is precisely in the clear distinction between them that their oneness becomes apparent.

—from *Life Together* 74–75

Working toward God

Work puts human beings in the world of things. It requires achievement from them. Christians step out of the world of personal encounter into the world of impersonal things, the "It"; and this new encounter frees them for objectivity, for the world of the It is only an instrument in the hands of God for the purification of Christians from all self-absorption and selfishness. The work of the world can only be accomplished where people forget themselves, where they lose themselves in a cause, reality, the task, the It. Christians learn at work to allow the task to set the bounds for them. Thus, for them, work becomes a remedy for the lethargy and laziness of the flesh. The demands of the flesh die in the world of things. But that can only happen where Christians break through the It to the "You" of God, who commands the work and the deed and makes them serve to liberate Christians from themselves.

—from *Life Together* 75

Good Work

In this process work does not cease to be work; but the severity and rigor of labor is sought all the more by those who know what good it does them. The continuing conflict with the It remains. But at the same time the breakthrough has been made. The unity of prayer and work, the unity of the day, is found because finding the You of God behind the It of the day's work is what Paul means by his admonition to "pray without ceasing" (1 Thess. 5:17). The prayer of the Christian reaches, therefore, beyond the time allocated to it and extends into the midst of the work. It surrounds the whole day, and in so doing it does not hinder work; it promotes work, affirms work, gives work great significance and joyfulness. Thus every word, every deed, every piece of work of the Christian becomes a prayer....

—from *Life Together* 75–76

Strength for the Day

Prayer offered in early morning is decisive for the day. The wasted time we are ashamed of, the temptations we succumb to, the weakness and discouragement in our work, the disorder and lack of discipline in our thinking and in our dealings with other people—all these very frequently have their cause in our neglect of morning prayer. The ordering and scheduling of our time will become more secure when it comes from prayer. The temptations of the working day will be overcome by this breakthrough to God. The decisions that are demanded by our work will become simpler and easier when they are made not in fear of other people, but solely before the face of God. "Whatever you do, do it from your hearts, as done for the Lord and not done for human beings" (Col. 3:23). Even routine mechanical work will be performed more patiently when it comes from the knowledge of God and God's command. Our strength and energy for work increase when we have asked God to give us the strength we need for our daily work.

—from *Life Together* 76

March

Driven to Prayer

When I think of you every morning and evening, I have to try very hard not to let all my thoughts dwell on the many cares and anxieties that beset you, instead of praying for you properly. . . . Psalm 50 says quite clearly, "Call upon me in the day of trouble; I will deliver you, and you shall glorify me." The whole history of the children of Israel consists of such cries for help. And I must say that the last two nights have made me face this problem again in a quite elementary way. While the bombs are falling like that all round the building, I cannot help thinking of God, his judgment, his hand stretched out, and his anger not turned away (Is. 5:25 and 9:11–10:4), and of my own unpreparedness. I feel how men can make vows, and then I think of you all and say, "better me than one of them"—and that makes me realize how attached I am to you all. I won't say anything more about it—it will have to be by word of mouth; but when all is said and done, it is true that it needs trouble to shake us up and drive us to prayer, though I feel every time that it is something to be ashamed of, as indeed it is.

—from *Letters and Papers from Prison* 106–107

Who Can Be Saved?

"Then Jesus said to his disciples, 'Truly I tell you, it will be hard for a rich person to enter the kingdom of heaven. Again I tell you, it is easier for a camel to go through the eye of a needle than for someone who is rich to enter the kingdom of God.' When the disciples heard this, they were greatly astounded and said, 'Then who can be saved?' But Jesus looked at them and said, 'For mortals it is impossible, for God all things are possible' " (Matt. 19:23–26). It can be inferred from the perplexity of the disciples about Jesus's word and from their question—"Who, then, can be saved?"—that they believe that the case of the rich young man is not an individual case, but the most general case possible. They do not ask, "Which rich person?" Instead, they ask the general question, "Who, then, can be saved?" This is because everyone, even the disciples, forms part of those rich people, for whom it is so difficult to enter heaven. Jesus's answer confirms this interpretation of his words by his disciples. Being saved by discipleship is not a human possibility, but for God all things are possible.

—from *Discipleship* 83

The Call of Grace

When Faust says at the end of his life of seeking knowledge, "I see that we can know nothing," then that is a conclusion, a result. It is something entirely different than when a student repeats this statement in the first semester to justify his laziness (Kierkegaard). Used as a conclusion, the sentence is true; as a presupposition, it is self-deception. That means that knowledge cannot be separated from the existence in which it was acquired. Only those who in following Christ leave everything they have can stand and say that they are justified solely by grace. They recognize the call to discipleship itself as grace and grace as that call. But those who want to use this grace to excuse themselves from discipleship are deceiving themselves.

—from *Discipleship* 51

By The Powers for Good

May your waxen candles flaming spread their warmth,
As their glow flickers darkness into the light.
May your will be done to make us one again;
May your love's glimmering hope illumine our night.

When now the silence spreads around us,
O let us hear the sounds you raise,
Of world unseen in growth abounding,
And the children chanting hymns of praise.

The forces for good surround us in wonder,
They firm up our courage for what comes our way,
God's with us from dawn to the slumber of evening,
The promise of love at break of each day.

—from *A Testament to Freedom* 522

Peace in Suffering

The test of whether we have truly found the peace of God will be in how we face the sufferings which befall us. There are many Christians who bend their knees before the cross of Jesus Christ well enough, but who do nothing but resist and struggle against every affliction in their own lives. They believe that they love Christ's cross, but they hate the cross in their own lives. In reality, therefore, they hate the cross of Jesus Christ as well; in reality, they are despisers of the cross, who for their part, seek to flee the cross by whatever means they can. Whoever regards suffering and trouble in their own life as something wholly hostile, wholly evil, can know by this that they have not yet found peace with God at all. Actually, they have only sought peace with the world, thinking perhaps that they could cope with themselves and all their questions with the cross of Jesus Christ; in other words, that the could find inner peace of mind. Thus, they needed the cross, but did not love it. They sought peace only for their own sake. When sufferings come, however, this peace quickly disappears. It was no peace with God because they hated the sufferings God sends. . . . Whoever loves the cross of Jesus Christ, whoever has found peace in him, they begin to love even the sufferings in their life, and in the end, they will be able to say with Scripture, "We also rejoice in our sufferings."

—from *A Testament to Freedom* 291

Remaining Underneath

Perseverance, translated literally, means: remaining underneath, not throwing off the load, but bearing it. We know much too little in the church today about the peculiar blessing of bearing. Bearing, not shaking off; bearing, but not collapsing either; bearing as Christ bore the cross, remaining underneath, and there beneath it—to find Christ. If God imposes a load; then those who persevere bow their heads and believe that it is good for them to be humbled—remain *underneath!* But *remaining* underneath. For remaining steadfast, remaining strong is meant here too; not weak acquiescence or surrender, not masochism, but growing stronger under the load, as under God's grace, imperturbably preserving the peace of God. God's peace is found with those who persevere.

—from *A Testament to Freedom* 291

Seeking Peace

A Christian life proves itself not in words, but character. No one is a Christian without character. . . . Only those who persevere are experienced and produce character. Those who do not persevere experience nothing that will build character. To whomever God wants to grant such experience—to an individual or to a church—to them God sends much temptation, restlessness, and anxiety; they must cry out daily and hourly for the peace of God. The experience that is talked of here leads us into the depths of hell, to the jaws of death, and into the night of unbelief. But through all of that, God does not want to take God's peace from us. Throughout, we experience God's power and victory, and the ultimate peace at Christ's cross more with each passing day.

—from *A Testament to Freedom* 292

Victory!

In our lives we don't speak readily of victory. It is too big a word for us. We have suffered too many defeats in our lives; victory has been thwarted again and again by too many weak hours, too many gross sins. But isn't it true that the spirit within us yearns for this word, for the final victory over the sin and anxious fear of death in our lives? And now God's Word also says nothing to us about our victory; it doesn't promise us that *we* will be victorious over sin and death from now on; rather, it says with all its might that someone has won this victory, and that this person, if we have him as Lord, will also win the victory over us. It is not we who are victorious, but Jesus. We proclaim that today and believe it despite all that we see around us, despite the graves of our loved ones, despite the moribund nature outside, despite the death that the war brings upon us again. We see the supremacy of death; yet we proclaim and believe the victory of Jesus Christ over death. Death is swallowed up in victory. Jesus is the victor, the resurrection of the dead, and the everlasting life.

—from *A Testament to Freedom* 298–299

The Idolization of Death

The miracle of Christ's resurrection has overturned the idolization of death that rules among us. Where death is final, fear of it combines with defiance. Where death is final, earthly life is all or nothing. Defiant striving for earthly eternities goes together with a careless playing with life, anxious affirmation of life with an indifferent contempt for life. Nothing betrays the idolization of death more clearly than when an era claims to build for eternity, and yet life in that era is worth nothing, when big words are spoken about a new humanity, a new world, a new society that will be created, and all this newness consists only in the annihilation of existing life. The radicality of this Yes and No to earthly life reveals that only death counts. To rake in everything or to throw away everything, this is the attitude of one who believes fanatically in death.

—from *Ethics* 91–92

The New Humanity

Where it is recognized that the power of death has been broken, where the miracle of the resurrection and new life shines right into the world of death, there one demands no eternities from life. One takes from life what it offers, not all or nothing, but good things and bad, important things and unimportant, joy and pain. One doesn't cling anxiously to life, but neither does one throw it lightly away. One is content with measured time and does not attribute eternity to earthly things. One leaves to death the limited right that it still has. But one expects the new human being and the new world only from beyond death, from the power that has conquered death. Within the risen Christ the new humanity is borne, the final, sovereign Yes of God to the new human being. Humanity still lives, of course, in the old, but is already beyond the old. Humanity still lives, of course, in a world of death, but is already beyond death. Humanity still lives, of course, in a world of sin, but we are already beyond sin. The night is not yet over, but day is already dawning.

—from *Ethics* 92

Fueling Evil

The only way to overcome evil is to let it run itself to a standstill because it does not find the resistance it is looking for. Resistance merely creates further evil and adds fuel to the flames. But when evil meets no opposition and encounters no obstacle but only patient endurance, its sting is drawn, and at last it meets an opponent which is more than its match. Of course this can only happen when the last ounce of resistance is abandoned, and the renunciation of revenge is complete. Then evil cannot find its mark, it can breed no further evil, and is left barren.

—from *A Testament to Freedom* 317

Enduring Evil

By willing endurance we cause suffering to pass. Evil becomes a spent force when we put up no resistance. By refusing to pay back the enemy in his own coin, and by preferring to suffer without resistance, the Christian exhibits the sinfulness of contumely and insult. Violence stands condemned by its failure to evoke counter-violence. When a man unjustly demands that I should give him my coat, I offer him my cloak also, and so counter his demand; when he requires me to go the other mile, I go willingly, and show up his exploitation of my service for what it is. To leave everything behind at the call of Christ is to be content with him alone, and to follow only him. By their willingly renouncing self-defense, Christians affirm their absolute adherence to Jesus, and their freedom from the tyranny of their own ego. The exclusiveness of this adherence is the only power which can overcome evil.

—from *A Testament to Freedom* 317

Death to Evil

We are concerned not with evil in the abstract, but with the evil *person*. Jesus bluntly calls the evil person evil. If I am assailed, I am not to condone or justify aggression. Patient endurance of evil does not mean a recognition of its rights. That is sheer sentimentality, and Jesus will a have nothing to do with it. The shameful assault, the deed of violence and the act of exploitation are still evil. The disciple must realize this, and bear witness to it as Jesus did, just because this is the only way evil can be met and overcome. The very fact that the evil which assaults them is unjustifiable makes it imperative that they should not resist it, but play it out and overcome it by patiently enduring the evil person. Suffering willingly endured is stronger than evil, it spells death to evil.

—from *A Testament to Freedom* 317

The Precept of Nonviolence

The Reformers offered a decisively new interpretation of [the Sermon on the Mount] and contributed a new idea of paramount importance. They distinguished between personal sufferings and those incurred by Christians in the performance of duty as bearers of an office ordained by God, maintaining that the precept of nonviolence applies to the first but not to the second. In the second case we are not only freed from obligation to eschew violence, but if we want to act in a genuine spirit of love we must do the very opposite and meet force with force in order to check the assault of evil. It was along these lines that the Reformers justified war and other legal sanctions against evil. But this distinction between person and office is wholly alien to the teaching of Jesus. He says nothing about that. He addresses his disciples as people who have left all to follow him, and the precept of nonviolence applies equally to private life and official duty. He is the Lord of all life and demands undivided allegiance.

—from *A Testament to Freedom* 317–318

Impracticable Jesus?

How then can the precept of Jesus be justified in the light of experience? It is obvious that weakness and defenselessness only invite aggression. Is then the demand of Jesus nothing but an impracticable ideal? Does he refuse to face up to realities—or shall we say, to the sin of the world? There may of course be a legitimate place for such an ideal in the inner life of the Christian community, but in the outside world such an ideal appears to wear the blinkers of perfectionism, and to take no account of sin. Living as we do in a world of sin and evil, we can have no truck with anything as impracticable as that. Jesus, however, tells us that it is just *because* we live in the world, and just *because* the world is evil, that the precept of nonresistance must be put into practice.

—from *A Testament to Freedom* 318

Nonviolence and the Cross

Surely we do not wish to accuse Jesus of ignoring the reality and power of evil! Why the whole of his life was one long conflict with the devil. He calls evil evil, and that is the very reason why he speaks to his followers in this way. How is that possible? If we took the precept of nonresistance as an ethical blueprint for general application, we should indeed be indulging in idealistic dreams: we should be dreaming of a utopia with laws which the world would never obey. To make nonresistance a principle for secular life is to deny God, by undermining God's gracious ordinance for the preservation of the world. But Jesus is no draftsman of political blueprints; he is the one who vanquished evil through suffering. It looked as though evil had triumphed on the cross, but the real victory belonged to Jesus. And the cross is the only justification for the precept of nonviolence, for it alone can kindle a faith in the victory over evil which will enable people to obey that precept. And only such obedience is blessed with the promise that we shall be partakers of Christ's victory as well as of his sufferings.

—from *A Testament to Freedom* 318

Love's Victory

The passion of Christ is the victory of divine love over the powers of evil, and therefore it is the only supportable basis for Christian obedience. Once again, Jesus calls those who follow him to share his passion. How can we convince the world by our preaching of the passion when we shrink from that passion in our own lives? On the cross Jesus fulfilled the law he himself established and thus graciously keeps his disciples in the community of his suffering. The cross is the only power in the world which proves that suffering love can avenge and vanquish evil. But it was just this participation in the cross which the disciples were granted when Jesus called them to him. They are called blessed because of their visible participation in his cross.

—from *A Testament to Freedom* 318–319

Standing with the Enemy

"Pray for those who hate and persecute you." This is the supreme demand. Through the medium of prayer we go to our enemies, stand by their side, and plead for them to God. Jesus does not promise that when we bless our enemies and do good to them they will not despitefully use and persecute us. They certainly will. But not even that can hurt or overcome us, so long as we pray for them. For if we pray for them, we are taking their distress and poverty, their guilt and perdition, upon ourselves, and pleading to God for them. We are doing vicariously for them what they cannot do for themselves. Every insult they utter only serves to bind us more closely to God and them. Their persecution of us only serves to bring them nearer to reconciliation with God and to further the triumphs of love.

—from *A Testament to Freedom* 319

Love versus Hate

How then does love conquer? By asking not how the enemy treats love but only how Jesus treated it. The love for our enemies takes us along the way of the cross and into the community with the crucified. The more we are driven along this road, the more certain is the victory of love over the enemy's hatred. For then it is not the disciple's own love, but the love of Jesus Christ alone, who for the sake of his enemies went to the cross and prayed for them as he hung there. In the face of the cross the disciples realized that they too were his enemies and that he had overcome them by his love. It is this that opens the disciples' eyes and enables them to see their enemy as a brother or sister. They know that they owe their very life to One who, though he was their enemy, accepted them, who made them his neighbors, and drew them into community with himself. The disciples can now perceive that even their enemies are the object of God's love, and that they stand like themselves beneath the cross of Christ.

—from *A Testament to Freedom* 319

The Holy Struggle

This commandment, that we should love our enemies and forgo revenge, will grow even more urgent in the holy struggle which lies before us and in which we partly have already been engaged for years. In it love and hate engage in mortal combat. It is the urgent duty of every Christian soul to prepare itself for it. The time is coming when the confession of the living God will incur not only the hatred and the fury of the world, for on the whole it has come to that already, but complete ostracism from "human society" as they call it. The Christians will be hounded from place to place, subjected to physical assault, maltreatment, and death of every kind. We are approaching an age of widespread persecution. Therein lies the true significance of all the movements and conflicts of our age. Our adversaries seek to root out the Christian Church and the Christian faith because they cannot live side by side with us, because they see in every word we utter and every deed we do, even when they are not specifically directed against them, a condemnation of their own words and deeds. They are not far wrong.

—from *A Testament to Freedom* 319–320

The Prayer of Love

We do not reciprocate . . . hatred and contention, although [our enemies] would like it better if we did, and so sink to their own level. And how is the battle to be fought? Soon the time will come when we shall pray, not as isolated individuals, but as a corporate body, a congregation, a church: we shall pray in multitudes (albeit relatively small multitudes) and among the thousands and thousands of apostates we shall loudly praise and confess the Lord who was crucified and is risen and shall come again. And what prayer, what confession, what hymn of praise will it be? It will be the prayer of earnest love for these very children of perdition who stand around and gaze at us with eyes aflame with hatred, and who have perhaps already raised their hands to kill us. It will be prayer for the peace of these erring, devastated, and bewildered souls, a prayer which will penetrate to the depths of their souls and rend their hearts more grievously than anything they can do to us. Yes, the church which is really waiting for its Lord, and which discerns the signs of the times of decision, must fling itself with its utmost power and with the panoply of its holy life into this prayer of love.

—from *A Testament to Freedom* 320

Undivided Love

What is undivided love? Love which shows no special favor to those who love us in return. When we love those who love us, our brethren, our nation, our friends, yes, and even our own congregation, we are no better than the heathen and the publicans. Such love is ordinary and natural, and not distinctively Christian. We can love our kith and kin, our fellow countrymen and our friends, whether we are Christians or not, and there is no need for Jesus to teach us that. But he takes that kind of love for granted, and in contrast asserts that we must love our enemies. Thus he shows us what *he* means by love, and the attitude we must display toward it.

—from *A Testament to Freedom* 320

Penultimate Things

The justifying word of God is . . . the *temporally* ultimate word. Something penultimate always precedes it, some action, suffering, movement, intention, defeat, recovery, pleading, hoping—in short, quite literally a span of time at whose end it stands. The only thing that can be justified is something that has already come under indictment in time. Justification presupposes that the creature became guilty. Not all time is a time of grace; but now—precisely now and finally now—is the "day of salvation" (2 Cor. 6:2). The time of grace is the final time in the sense that one can never reckon with a further, future word beyond the word of God that confronts me now. There is a time of God's permission, waiting, and preparation; and there is an ultimate time that judges and breaks off the penultimate. In order to hear the ultimate word, Luther had to go through the monastery; Paul had to go through his piety toward the law; even the thief "had to" go through conviction and the cross. They had to travel a road, to walk the full length of the way through penultimate things; they had to sink to their knees under the burden of these things. And yet the ultimate word was not a crowning but a complete break with the penultimate.

—from *Ethics* 150–151

The Ultimate Word

Before the ultimate word Luther and Paul stood no differently than the thief on the cross. We must travel a road, even though there is no road to this goal, and we must travel this road to the end, that is, to the place where God puts an end to it. The penultimate remains in existence, even though it is completely superseded by the ultimate and is no longer in force. The word of God's justifying grace never leaves its place as the ultimate word. It never simply presents itself as an achieved outcome that could now just as well be placed at the beginning as at the end. The way from the penultimate to the ultimate cannot be abandoned. The word remains irreversibly the ultimate; otherwise it would be degraded to something calculable, a commodity, and would be robbed of its essential divinity. Grace would become cheap; it would not be a gift.

—from *Ethics* 151

Human Reality

Jesus Christ the human being—that means that God enters into created reality, that we may be and should be human beings before God. The destruction of humanness is sin, and as such it hinders God's work of redeeming humanity. Still, Jesus Christ's being human does not mean simply the confirmation of the existing world and of human existence. Jesus was human "without sin" (Heb. 4:15); that is the decisive thing. But Jesus lived among us in deepest poverty, was unmarried, and died as a criminal. Jesus's being human embodies therefore a double judgment on human beings—the absolute condemnation of sin and the relative condemnation of existing human orders. Included in this condemnation, however, is that Jesus is really human and wants us to be human beings. Jesus lets human reality exist as penultimate, neither making it self-sufficient nor destroying it—a penultimate that will be taken seriously and not seriously in its own way, a penultimate that has become the cover of the ultimate.

—from *Ethics* 157–158

Serious Discipleship

If our Christianity has ceased to be serious about discipleship, if we have watered down the gospel into emotional uplift which makes no costly demands and which fails to distinguish between natural and Christian existence, then we cannot help regarding the cross as an ordinary everyday calamity, as one of the trials and tribulations of life. We have then forgotten that the cross means rejection and shame as well as suffering. The psalmist was lamenting that he was despised and rejected . . . and that is an essential quality of the suffering of the cross. But this notion has ceased to be intelligible to a Christianity which can no longer see any difference between an ordinary human life and a life committed to Christ. The cross means sharing the suffering of Christ to the last and to the fullest. Only those thus totally committed in discipleship can experience the meaning of the cross.

—from *A Testament to Freedom* 313

Pick Up Your Cross

The cross is there, right from the beginning, [we] have only got to pick it up; there is no need for [us] to go out and look for a cross for [ourselves], no need for [us] deliberately to run after suffering. Jesus says that all Christians have their own crosses waiting for them, a cross destined and appointed by God. Each of us must endure our allotted share of suffering and rejection. But each of us has a different share: some God deems worthy of the highest form of suffering, and gives them the grace of martyrdom, while others God does not allow to be tempted above what they are able to bear. But it is the one and the same cross in every case.

—from *A Testament to Freedom* 313

Every Christian's Cross

The cross is laid on every Christian. The first Christ-suffering which every person must experience is the call to abandon the attachments of this world. It is that dying of the old person which is the result of our encounter with Christ. As we embark upon discipleship we surrender ourselves to Christ in union with his death—we give over our lives to death. Thus it begins; the cross is not the terrible end to an otherwise God-fearing and happy life, but it meets us at the beginning of our communion with Christ. When Christ calls us, he bids us come and die. It may be a death like that of the first disciples who had to leave home and work to follow him, or it may be a death like Luther's, who had to leave the monastery and go out into the world. But it is the same death every time—death in Jesus Christ, the death of the old person at his call.

—from *A Testament to Freedom* 313

The Call to Die

Jesus's summons to the rich young man was calling him to die, because only we who are dead to our own will can follow Christ. In fact every command of Jesus is a call to die, with all our affections and lusts. But we do not want to die, and therefore Jesus Christ and his call are necessarily our death as well as our life. The call to discipleship, the baptism in the name of Jesus Christ, means both death and life. The call of Christ, his baptism, sets the Christian in the middle of the daily arena against sin and the devil. Every day we encounter new temptations, and every day we must suffer anew for Jesus Christ's sake. The wounds and scars we receive in the fray are living tokens of this participation in the cross of our Lord.

—from *A Testament to Freedom* 314

God's Final Judgment

Jesus Christ the crucified—that means that God speaks final judgment on the fallen creation. The rejection of the whole human race without exception is included in the rejection of God on the cross of Jesus Christ. Jesus's cross is the death sentence on the world. Here human beings cannot boast of their being human, nor the world of its divine orders. Here human glory has come to its final end in the image of the beaten, bleeding, spat-upon face of the crucified. Yet the crucifixion of Jesus does not mean simply the annihilation of creation. Human beings will live on under this death-sign of the cross, living on toward judgment when they despise it, but living on toward salvation when they accept it. The ultimate has become real in the cross—as judgment on all that is penultimate, but at the same time as grace for the penultimate that bows to the judgment of the ultimate.

—from *Ethics* 158

The End of Death

Jesus Christ the resurrected—that means that God, in love and omnipotence, makes an end of death and calls a new creation into life. God gives new life. "The old has gone." "See, I am making all things new." The resurrection has already broken into the midst of the old world as the ultimate sign of its end and its future, and at the same time as living reality. Jesus has risen as human; so he has given human beings the gift of resurrection. Thus human beings remain human, but in a new resurrected way that is completely unlike the old. To be sure, those who are already risen with Christ will remain, until they reach the frontier of death, in the world of the penultimate to which Jesus came and in which the cross stands. Even the resurrection does not abolish the penultimate as long as the earth remains; but eternal life, the new life, breaks even more powerfully into earthly life and creates space for itself within it. The unity and differentiation of incarnation, cross, and resurrection should be clear. Christian life is life with Jesus Christ who became human, was crucified, and is risen, and whose word as a whole encounters us in the message of the justification of the sinner by grace. Christian life means being human in the power of Christ's becoming human, being judged and pardoned in the power of the cross, living a new life in the power of the resurrection. No one of these is without the others.

—from *Ethics* 158–159

April

Stronger Hands

As long as we ourselves are trying to help shape someone else's destiny, we are never quite free of the question whether what we are doing is really for the other person's benefit—at least in any matter of great importance. But when all possibility of cooperating in anything is suddenly cut off, then behind any anxiety about him there is the consciousness that his life has now been placed wholly in better and stronger hands. For you, and for us, the greatest task during the coming weeks, and perhaps months, may be to entrust each other to those hands. Whatever weaknesses, miscalculations, and guilt there is in what precedes the facts, God is in the facts themselves.

—from *Letters and Papers from Prison* 102–103

Finding Meaning

In these turbulent times we repeatedly lose sight of what really makes life worth living. We think that, because this or that person is living, it makes sense for us to live too. But the truth is that if this earth was good enough for the man Jesus Christ, if such a man as Jesus lived, then, and only then, has life a meaning for us. If Jesus had not lived, then our life would be meaningless, in spite of all the other people whom we know and honor and love. Perhaps we now sometimes forget the meaning and purpose of our profession. But is not this the simplest way of putting it? The unbiblical idea of "meaning" is indeed only a translation of what the Bible calls "promise."

—from *Letters and Papers from Prison* 207

God in Christ

All that we may rightly expect from God, and ask God for, is to be found in Jesus Christ. The God of Jesus Christ has nothing to do with what God, as we imagine God, could do and ought to do. If we are to learn what God promises, and what God fulfils, we must persevere in quiet meditation on the life, sayings, deeds, sufferings, and death of Jesus. It is certain that we may always live close to God and in the light of God's presence, and that such living is an entirely new life for us; that nothing is then impossible for us, because all things are possible with God; that no earthly power can touch us without God's will, and that danger and distress can only drive us closer to God. It is certain that we can claim nothing for ourselves, and may yet pray for everything; it is certain that our joy is hidden in suffering, and our life in death; it is certain that in all this we are in a fellowship that sustains us. In Jesus God has said Yes and Amen to it all, and that Yes and Amen is the firm ground on which we stand.

—from *Letters and Papers from Prison* 206–207

Accepted by God

In the body of Jesus Christ, God is united with humankind, all humanity is accepted by God, and the world is reconciled to God. In the body of Jesus Christ, God took on the sin of the world and bore it. There is no part of the world, no matter how lost, no matter how godless, that has not been accepted by God in Jesus Christ and reconciled to God. Whoever perceives the body of Jesus Christ in faith can no longer speak of the world as if it were lost, as if it were separated from God; they can no longer separate themselves in clerical pride from the world. The world belongs to Christ, and only in Christ is the world what it is. It needs, therefore, nothing less than Christ himself. Everything would be spoiled if we were to reserve Christ for the church while granting the world only some law, Christian though it may be. Christ has died for the world, and Christ is Christ only in the midst of the world. It is nothing but unbelief to give the world . . . less than Christ. It means not taking seriously the incarnation, the crucifixion, and the bodily resurrection. It means denying the body of Christ.

—from *Ethics* 66–67

Set Apart

When the New Testament transfers the concept of the body of Christ to the church-community, this is in no way an expression that the church-community is first and foremost set apart from the world. On the contrary, in line with New Testament statements about God becoming flesh in Christ, it expresses just this—that in the body of Christ all humanity is accepted, included, and borne, and that the church-community of believers is to make this known to the world by word and life. This means not being separated from the world, but calling the world into the community of the body of Christ to which the world in truth already belongs. This witness is strange to the world, and in giving this witness the church-community experiences itself as strange to the world. Yet such strangeness is a consequence that ever and again follows from the communion that the body of Christ has with the world. The church-community is separated from the world only by this: it believes in the reality of being accepted by God—a reality that belongs to the whole world—and in affirming this as valid for itself it witnesses that it is valid for the entire world.

—from *Ethics* 67–68

On April 5, 1943, Bonhoeffer is arrested and incarcerated at Tegel Prison in Berlin.

God in Our Midst

Now in Jesus Christ this is just what has happened. The image of God has entered our midst, in the form of our fallen life, in the likeness of sinful flesh. In the teaching and acts of Christ, in his life and death, the image of God is revealed. In him the divine image has been re-created on earth. The Incarnation, the words and acts of Jesus, his death on the cross, are all indispensable parts of that image. But it is not the same image as Adam bore in the primal glory of paradise. Rather, it is the image of one who enters a world of sin and death, who takes upon himself all the sorrows of humanity, who meekly bears God's wrath and judgment against sinners, and obeys God's will with unswerving devotion in suffering and death, the man born to poverty, the friend of publicans and sinners, the man of sorrows, rejected by people and forsaken of God. Here is God made human, here is the human in the new image of God.

—from *A Testament to Freedom* 320–321

Marks of Grace

We know full well that the marks of the passion, the wounds of the cross, are now become the marks of grace in the body of the risen and glorified Christ. We know that the image of the Crucified lives henceforth in the glory of the eternal High Priest, who ever makes intercession for us in heaven. That body, in which Christ had lived in the form of a servant, rose on Easter Day as a new body, with heavenly form and radiance. But if we would have a share in that glory and radiance, we must first be conformed to the image of the Suffering Servant who was obedient to the death of the cross. If we would bear the image of his glory, we must first bear the image of his shame. There is no other way to recover the image we lost through the Fall.

—from *A Testament to Freedom* 321

God's Vengeance

Jesus Christ died the death of the ungodly, struck down by God's wrath and vengeance. His blood is the blood God's justice demanded for the transgression of God's commandments. God's vengeance has been carried out right here on earth, more terribly than the psalmist himself knows. Christ, the innocent one, died the death of a sinner so that we do not have to die. Now we stand as sinners at the foot of his cross and now a puzzle difficult to understand is solved: Jesus Christ, the innocent one, prays as God's vengeance on the godless is fulfilled, he prays as [Psalm 58] is fulfilled: "Father, forgive them for they know not what they do" (Luke 23:24). The one who bore the vengeance, he alone was allowed to ask for the forgiveness of the godless. He alone has set us free from God's wrath and revenge; he has brought forgiveness to his enemies and no one before him was allowed to pray like that. He alone is allowed to. If we look at him, the crucified one, we recognize God's true and living anger at us godless and the same moment, our liberation from this anger, and we hear, "Father, forgive them for they know not what they do." . . . God's vengeance has died and the blood of the godless one in whom we bathe ourselves gives us a share in God's victory; the blood of the godless one has become our redemption, it cleanses us of all our sin. That is the miracle.

—from *A Testament to Freedom* 281–282

The Prize

We realize more clearly than formerly that the world lies under the wrath and grace of God. We read in Jeremiah 45: "Thus says the Lord: Behold, what I have built I am breaking down, and what I have planted I am plucking up. . . . And do you seek great things for yourself? Seek them not; for, behold, I am bringing evil upon all flesh . . . but I will give your life as a prize of war in all places to which you may go." If we can save our souls unscathed out of the wreckage of our material possessions, let us be satisfied with that. If the Creator destroys the Divine handiwork, what right have we to lament the destruction of ours? It will be the task of our generation, not to "seek great things," but to save and preserve our souls out of the chaos, and to realize that it is the only thing we can carry as a "prize" from the burning building.

—from *Letters and Papers from Prison* 157–158

On April 9, 1945, Bonhoeffer is executed at Flossenburg along with other members of the resistance.

Knowing Death

Who understands the choice of those whom God takes to the divine self early? Does it not seem to us again and again in the early deaths of Christians as though God were robbing the divine self of God's best instruments at a time when God needed them most? But God makes no mistakes. Does God perhaps need our brothers and sisters for some hidden service for us in the heavenly world? We should restrain our human thoughts, which always seek to know more than they can, and keep to what is certain. God has loved anyone whom God has called. "For his soul was pleasing to the Lord, therefore he took him quickly from the midst of wickedness" (Wisd. of Sol. 4:14).

—from *A Testament to Freedom* 454

God's Will

We know that God and the devil are locked together in combat over the world and that the devil has a word to say even at death. In the face of death we cannot say in a fatalistic way, "It is God's will"; we must add the opposite: "It is not God's will." Death shows that the world is not what it should be, but that it needs redemption. Christ alone overcomes death. Here, "It is God's will" and "It is not God's will" come to the most acute paradox and balance each other out. God agrees to be involved in something that is not the divine will, and from now on death must serve God despite itself. From now on, "It is God's will" also embraces "It is not God's will." God's will is the overcoming of death through the death of Jesus Christ. Only in the cross and resurrection of Jesus Christ has death come under God's power, must it serve the purpose of God. Not a fatalistic surrender, but living faith in Jesus Christ, who died and has risen again for us, can seriously make an end of death for us.

—from *A Testament to Freedom* 454–455

Death Comes Again

Death has again come among us, and we must think about it, whether we want to or not. Two things have become important to me recently: death is outside us, and it is in us. Death from outside is the fearful foe which comes to us when it will. It is the man with the scythe, under whose stroke the blossoms fall. It guides the bullet that goes home. We can do nothing against it, "it has power from the supreme God." It is the death of the whole human race, God's wrath, and the end of all life. But the other is death in us, it is our own death. That too has been in us since the fall of Adam. But it belongs to us. We die daily to it in Jesus Christ or we deny him. This death in us has something to do with love toward Christ and toward people. We die to it when we love Christ and the brethren from the bottom of our hearts, for love is total surrender to what a person loves. This death is grace and the consummation of love. It should be our prayer that we die this death, that it be sent to us, that death only comes to us from outside when we have been made ready for it by this our own death. For our death is really only the way to the perfect love of God.

—from *A Testament to Freedom* 447

The Peacemakers

When fighting and death exercise their wild dominion around us, then we are called to bear witness to God's love and God's peace not only by word and thought, but also by our deeds. Read James 4:1ff! We should daily ask ourselves where we can bear witness in what we do to the kingdom in which love and peace prevail. The great peace for which we long can only grow again from peace between twos and threes. Let us put an end to all hate, mistrust, envy, disquiet, wherever we can. "Blessed are the peacemakers, for they shall be called the children of God."

—from *A Testament to Freedom* 447–448

Dying and Death

Easter? We are paying more attention to dying than to death. We are more concerned to get over the act of dying than to overcome death. Socrates mastered the art of dying; Christ overcame death as "the last enemy" (1 Cor. 15:26). There is a real difference between the two things; the one is within the scope of human possibilities, the other means resurrection. It is not from *ars moriendi,* the art of dying, but from the resurrection of Christ, that a new and purifying wind can blow through our present world. *Here* is the answer to "Give me a place to stand and I will move the earth." If a few people really believed that and acted on it in their daily lives, a great deal would be changed. To live in the light of the resurrection—that is what Easter means. Do you find, too, that most people do not know what they really live by? . . . It is an unconscious waiting for the word of deliverance, though the time is probably not yet ripe for it to be heart. But the time will come, and this Easter may be one of our last chances to prepare ourselves for our great task of the future.

—from *Letters and Papers from Prison* 132–133

Love Really Lived

In Christ the reconciliation of the world with God took place. The world will be overcome not by destruction but by reconciliation. Not ideals or programs, not conscience, duty, responsibility, or virtue, but only the consummate love of God can meet and overcome reality. Again, this is accomplished not by a general idea of love, but by the love of God really lived in Jesus Christ. This love of God for the world does not withdraw from reality into noble souls detached from the world, but experiences and suffers the reality of the world at its worst. The world exhausts its rage on the body of Jesus Christ. But the martyred one forgives the world its sins. Thus reconciliation takes place.

—from *Ethics* 82–83

The Pious Community

"Confess your sins to one another" (James 5:16). Those who remain alone with their evil are left utterly alone. It is possible that Christians may remain lonely in spite of daily worship together, prayer together, and all their community through service—that the final breakthrough to community does not occur precisely because they enjoy community with one another as pious believers, but not with one another as those lacking piety, as sinners. For the pious community permits no one to be a sinner. Hence all have to conceal their sins from themselves and from the community. We are not allowed to be sinners. Many Christians would be unimaginably horrified if a real sinner were suddenly to turn up among the pious. So we remain alone with our sin, trapped in lies and hypocrisy, for we are in fact sinners.

—from *Life Together* 108

Unholy Sinners

The grace of the gospel, which is so hard for the pious to comprehend, confronts us with the truth. It says to us, you are a sinner, a great, unholy sinner. Now come, as the sinner that you are, to your God who loves you. For God wants you as you are, not desiring anything from you—a sacrifice, a good deed—but rather desiring you alone. "My child, give me your heart" (Prov. 23:26). God has come to you to make the sinner blessed. Rejoice! This message is liberation through truth. You cannot hide from God. The mask you wear in the presence of other people won't get you anywhere in the presence of God. God wants to see you as you are, wants to be gracious to you. You do not have to go on lying to yourself and to other Christians as if you were without sin. You are allowed to be a sinner. Thank God for that.

—from *Life Together* 108

Christ Our Brother

Christ became our brother in the flesh in order that we might believe in him. In Christ, the love of God came to the sinner. In the presence of Christ human beings were allowed to be sinners, and only in this way could they be helped. Every pretense came to an end in Christ's presence. This was the truth of the gospel in Jesus Christ: the misery of the sinner and the mercy of God. The community of faith in Christ was to live in this truth. That is why Jesus gave his followers the authority to hear the confession of sin and to forgive sin in Christ's name. "If you forgive the sins of any, they are forgiven them; if you retain the sins of any, they are retained." (John 20:23). When he did that, Christ made us into the community of faith, and in that community Christ made the other Christian to be grace for us.

—from *Life Together* 109

Great Grace

Now each stands in Christ's place. In the presence of another Christian I no longer need to pretend. In another Christian's presence I am permitted to be the sinner that I am, for there alone in all the world the truth and mercy of Jesus Christ rule. Christ became our brother in order to help us; through Christ other Christians have become Christ for us in the power and authority of Christ's commandment. Other Christians stand before us as the sign of God's truth and grace. They have been given to us to help us. Another Christian hears our confession of sin in Christ's place, forgives our sins in Christ's name. Another Christian keeps the secret of our confession as God keeps it. When I go to another believer to confess, I am going to God. Thus the call within the Christian community to mutual confession and forgiveness goes out as a call to the great grace of God in the congregation.

—from *Life Together* 109

From Confession to Community

In confession there takes place a *breakthrough to community*. Sin wants to be alone with people. It takes them away from the community. The more lonely people become, the more destructive the power of sin over them. The more deeply they become entangled in it, the more unholy is their loneliness. Sin wants to remain unknown. It shuns the light. In the darkness of what is left unsaid sin poisons the whole being of a person. This can happen in the midst of a pious community. In confession the light of the gospel breaks into the darkness and closed isolation of the heart. Sin must be brought into the light. What is unspoken is said openly and confessed. All that is secret and hidden comes to light. It is a hard struggle until the sin crosses one's lips in confession. But God breaks down gates of bronze and cuts through bars of iron (Ps. 107:16). Since the confession of sin is made in the presence of another Christian, the last stronghold of self-justification is abandoned. The sinner surrenders, giving up all evil, giving the sinner's heart to God and finding the forgiveness of all one's sin in the community of Jesus Christ and other Christians.

—from *Life Together* 110

Sin Revealed

Sin that has been spoken and confessed has lost all of its power. It has been revealed and judged as sin. It can no longer tear apart the community. Now the community bears the sin of the individual believer, who is no longer alone with this evil but has "cast off" this sin by confessing it and handing it over to God. The sinner has been relieved of sin's burden. Now the sinner stands in the community of sinners who live by the grace of God in the cross of Jesus Christ. Now one is allowed to be a sinner and still enjoy the grace of God. We can admit our sins and in this very act find community for the first time. The hidden sins separated the sinner from the community and made the sinner's apparent community all a sham. The sins that were acknowledged helped the sinner to find true community with other believers in Jesus Christ.

—from *Life Together* 110

One on One

A confession of sin in the presence of all the members of the congregation is not required to restore one to community with the entire congregation. In the one other Christian to whom I confess my sins and by whom my sins are declared forgiven, I meet the whole congregation. Community with the whole congregation is given to me in the community which I experience with this one other believer. For here it is not a matter of acting according to one's own orders and authority, but according to the command of Jesus Christ, which is intended for the whole congregation, on whose behalf the individual is called merely to carry it out. So long as Christians are in such a community of confession of sins to one another, they are no longer alone anywhere.

—from *Life Together* 110–111

The Root of Sin

In confession there takes place a *breakthrough to the cross*. The root of all sin is pride. I want to be for myself; I have a right to be myself, a right to my hatred and my desires, my life and my death. The spirit and flesh of human beings are inflamed by pride, for it is precisely in their wickedness that human beings want to be like God. Confession in the presence of another believer is the most profound kind of humiliation. It hurts, makes one feel small; it deals a terrible blow to one's pride. To stand there before another Christian as a sinner is an almost unbearable disgrace. By confessing actual sins the old self dies a painful, humiliating death before the eyes of another Christian. Because this humiliation is so difficult, we keep thinking we can avoid confession to one another. Our eyes are so blinded that they no longer see the promise and the glory of such humiliation. It is none other than Jesus Christ who openly suffered the shameful death of a sinner in our place, who was not ashamed to be crucified for us as an evildoer. And it is nothing else but our community with Jesus Christ that leads us to the disgraceful dying that comes in confession so that we may truly share in this cross.

—from *Life Together* 111

On April 23, 1945, Bonhoeffer's brother and brother-in-law are killed in Berlin.

Shattering Sin

The cross of Jesus Christ shatters all pride. We cannot find the cross of Jesus if we are afraid of going to the place where Jesus can be found, to the public death of the sinner. And we refuse to carry the cross when we are ashamed to take upon ourselves the shameful death of the sinner in confession. In confession we break through to the genuine community of the cross of Jesus Christ; in confession we affirm our cross. In the profound spiritual and physical pain of humiliation before another believer, which means before God, we experience the cross of Jesus as our deliverance and salvation. The old humanity dies, but God has triumphed over it. Now we share in the resurrection of Christ and eternal life.

—from *Life Together* 111–112

The Just Judge

Why is it often easier for us to acknowledge our sins before God than before another believer? God is holy and without sin, a just judge of evil, and an enemy of all disobedience. But another Christian is sinful, as are we, knowing from personal experience the night of secret sin. Should we not find it easier to go to one another than to the holy God? But if that is not the case, we must ask ourselves whether we often have not been deluding ourselves about our confession of sin to God—whether we have not instead been confessing our sins to ourselves and also forgiving ourselves. And is not the reason for our innumerable relapses and for the feebleness of our Christian obedience to be found precisely in the fact that we are living from self-forgiveness and not from the real forgiveness of our sins? Self-forgiveness can never lead to the break with sin. This can only be accomplished by God's own judging and pardoning Word. Who can give us the assurance that we are not dealing with ourselves but with the living God in the confession and the forgiveness of our sins? God gives us this assurance through one another. The other believer breaks the circle of self-deception. Those who confess their sins in the presence of another Christian know that they are no longer alone with themselves; they experience the presence of God in the reality of the other.

—from *Life Together* 112–113

Divine Forgiveness

As long as I am by myself when I confess my sins, everything remains in the dark; but when I come face to face with another Christian, the sin has to be brought to light. But because the sin must come to light some time, it is better that it happens today between me and another believer, rather than on the last day in the bright light of the final judgment. It is grace that we can confess our sins to one another. Such grace spares us the terrors of the last judgment. The other Christian has been given to me so that I may be assured even here and now of the reality of God in judgment and grace. As the acknowledgment of my sins to another believer frees me from the grip of self-deception, so, too, the promise of forgiveness becomes fully certain to me only when it is spoken by another believer as God's command and in God's name. Confession before one another is given to us by God so that we may be assured of divine forgiveness.

—from *Life Together* 113

Concrete Confession

It is precisely for the sake of this assurance that confession is about admitting *concrete* sins. People usually justify themselves by making a general acknowledgment of sin. But I experience the complete forlornness and corruption of human nature, insofar as I ever experience it at all, when I see my own specific sins. Examining myself on the basis of all Ten Commandments will therefore be the right preparation for confession. Otherwise, it might happen that I could still become a hypocrite even in confessing to another Christian, and then God's comfort would continue to be remote from me. Jesus dealt with people whose sins were obvious, with tax collectors and prostitutes. They knew why they needed forgiveness, and they received it as forgiveness of their specific sins. Jesus asked blind Bartimaeus, "What do you want me to do for you?" (Luke 18:41). Before confession we must have a clear answer to this question. In confession we too receive the forgiveness of particular sins that come to light at that time. And it is in confessing these particular sins that we receive forgiveness of all our sins, both known and unknown.

—from *Life Together* 113–114

Necessary Help

It is possible that by God's grace a person may break through to assurance, new life, the cross, and community without benefit of confession to another believer. It is certainly possible that a person may never come to know what it means to doubt one's own forgiveness and question one's own confession of sin, that one may be given everything in one's solitary confession in the presence of God. We have spoken here for those who cannot say that about themselves. Luther himself was one of those for whom the Christian life was unthinkable without confession to one another. In *The Large Catechism* he said, "Therefore when I urge you to go to confession, I am urging you to be a Christian." The divine offer that is made to us in the form of confession to one another should be shown to all those who, despite all their searching and struggling, cannot find the great joy of community, the cross, the new life, and assurance. Confession stands in the realm of the freedom of the Christian. But who could, without suffering harm, turn down that help which God considered it necessary to offer?

—from *Life Together* 114

Living Beneath the Cross

Whoever lives beneath the cross of Jesus, and has discerned in the cross of Jesus the utter ungodliness of all people and of their own hearts, will find there is no sin that can ever be unfamiliar. Whoever has once been appalled by the horror of their own sin, which nailed Jesus to the cross, will no longer be appalled by even the most serious sin of another Christian; rather they know the human heart from the cross of Jesus. Such persons know how totally lost is the human heart in sin and weakness, how it goes astray in the ways of sin—and know too that this same heart is accepted in grace and mercy. Only another Christian who is under the cross can hear my confession. It is not experience with life but experience of the cross that makes one suited to hear confession. The most experienced judge of character knows infinitely less of the human heart than the simplest Christian who lives beneath the cross of Jesus. The greatest psychological insight, ability, and experience cannot comprehend this one thing: what sin is. Psychological wisdom knows what need and weakness and failure are, but it does not know the ungodliness of the human being. And so it also does not know that human beings are ruined only by their sin and are healed only by forgiveness. The Christian alone knows this.

—from *Life Together* 116

Confession and Communion

Although confession is an act in the name of Christ that is truly complete in itself and is practiced in the community as often as there is a desire for it, confession serves the Christian community especially as a preparation for participation together in the *Lord's Supper*. Reconciled to God and human beings, Christians desire to receive the body and blood of Jesus Christ. It is the command of Jesus that no one should come to the altar with a heart unreconciled to another Christian. If this command applies to all worship, indeed, to every prayer we offer, then it applies all the more to receiving the sacrament. The day before the Lord's Supper together will find the members of a Christian community with one another, each asking of the other forgiveness for wrongs committed. Anyone who avoids this path to another believer cannot go the table of the Lord well prepared. All anger, strife, envy, malicious gossip, and conduct to the detriment of one another must have been done away with if all wish to receive together the grace of God in the sacrament.

—from *Life Together* 116–117

On April 30, 1945, Adolf Hitler commits suicide in Berlin.

May

Joy in the Morning

What do we, who today no longer have any fear or awe of the darkness or night, know about the great joy that our forebears and the early Christians felt every morning at the return of the light? If we were to learn again something of the praise and adoration that is due the triune God early in the morning, then we would also begin to sense something of the joy that comes when night is past and those who dwell with one another come together early in the morning to praise their God and hear the Word and pray together. We would learn again of God the Father and Creator who has preserved our life through the dark night and awakened us to a new day; God the Son and Savior of the World, who vanquished death and hell for us, and dwells in our midst as Victor; God the Holy Spirit who pours the bright light of God's Word into our hearts early in the morning, driving away all darkness and sin and teaching us to pray the right way. Morning does not belong to the individual; it belongs to all the church of the triune God, to the community of Christians living together. . . .

—from *Life Together* 49

Awake!

For Christians the beginning of the day should not be burdened and haunted by the various kinds of concerns they face during the working day. The Lord stands above the new day, for God has made it. All the darkness and confusion of the night with its dreams gives way to the clear light of Jesus Christ and his awakening Word. All restlessness, all impurity, all worry and anxiety flee before him. Therefore, in the early morning hours of the day may our many thoughts and our many idle words be silent, and may the first thought and the first word belong to the one to whom our whole life belongs. "Sleeper, awake! Rise from the dead, and Christ will shine on you" (Eph. 5:14).

—from *Life Together* 51–52

On May 2, 1945, Berlin falls.

Christ in Us

To be conformed to the image of Christ is not an ideal to be striven after. It is not as though we had to imitate him as well as we could. We cannot transform ourselves into his image; it is rather the form of Christ which seeks to be formed in us (Gal. 4:19), and to be manifested in us. Christ's work in us is not finished until he has perfected his own form in us. We must be assimilated to the form of Christ in its entirety, the form of Christ incarnate, crucified, and glorified.

—from *A Testament to Freedom* 321

The Dignity of Humanity

Christ took upon himself this human form of ours. He became human even as we are men and women. In his humanity and his lowliness we recognize our own form. He has become like a man, so that people should be like him. And in the Incarnation the whole human race recovers the dignity of the image of God. Henceforth, any attack even on the least of people is an attack on Christ, who took human form, and in his own person restored the image of God in all that bears human form. Through community and communion with the incarnate Lord, we recover our humanity, and at the same time we are delivered from that individualism which is the consequence of sin, and retrieve our solidarity with the whole human race. By being partakers of Christ incarnate, we are partakers in the whole humanity which he bore.

—from *A Testament to Freedom* 321

The Body of Christ

We now know that we have been taken up and borne in the humanity of Jesus, and therefore that new nature we now enjoy means that we too much bear the sins and sorrows of others. The incarnate Lord makes his followers the brothers and sisters of all humanity. The "philanthropy" of God (Titus 3:4) revealed in the Incarnation is the ground of Christian love toward all on earth that bear the name of human. The form of Christ incarnate makes the church into the body of Christ. All the sorrows of humanity fall upon that form, and only through that form can they be borne. The earthly form of Christ is the form that died on the cross. The image of God is the image of Christ crucified. It is to this image that the life of the disciples must be conformed: in other words, they must be conformed to his death (Phil. 3:10; Rom. 6:4f). The Christian life is a life of crucifixion (Gal. 2:19).

—from *A Testament to Freedom* 321

Who Is Christ?

What is bothering me incessantly is the question what Christianity really is, or indeed who Christ really is, for us today. The time when people could be told everything by means of words, whether theological or pious, is over, and so is the time of inwardness and conscience—and that means the time of religion in general. We are moving toward a completely religionless time; people as they are now simply cannot be religious anymore. Even those who honestly describe themselves as "religious" do not in the least act up to it, and so they presumably mean something quite different by "religious." Our whole 1,900-year-old Christian preaching and theology rest on the "religious a priori" of humanity. "Christianity" has always been a form—perhaps the true form—of "religion." But if one day it becomes clear that this *a priori* does not exist at all, but was a historically conditioned and transient form of human self-expression, and if therefore people become radically religionless—and I think that that is already more or less the case (else how is it, for example, that this war, in contrast to all previous ones, is not calling forth any "religious" reaction?)—what does that mean for "Christianity"?

—from *A Testament to Freedom* 501

The Search for Authority

"Whoever wishes to become great among you must be your servant" (Mark 10:43). Jesus tied all authority in the community to service, one to another. Genuine spiritual authority is to be found only where the service of listening, helping, forbearing, and proclaiming is carried out. Every personality cult that bears the mark of the distinguished qualities, outstanding abilities, powers, and talents of another, even if these are of a thoroughly spiritual nature, is worldly and has no place in the Christian community of faith; indeed it poisons that community. The longing we so often hear expressed today for "episcopal figures," "priestly people," "authoritative personalities" often enough stems from a spiritually sick need to admire human beings and to establish visible human authority because the genuine authority of service appears to be too insignificant. Nothing contradicts such a desire more sharply than the New Testament itself in its description of a bishop (1 Tim. 3:1ff). None of the magic of human talents or the brilliant qualities of a spiritual personality is to be found there. Bishops are those unpretentious persons who are sound and loyal in faith and life and who properly carry out their ministry to the community of faith. The authority of bishops lies in accomplishing the tasks of their service. There is nothing to admire about the person himself.

—from *Life Together* 106

Genuine Authority

Ultimately, the craving for inauthentic authority reasserts its desire to reestablish some kind of immediacy, a commitment to a human figure in the church. Genuine authority knows, however, that all immediacy is disastrous, particularly in matters of authority. Genuine authority knows that it can only exist in the service of the One who alone has authority. Genuine authority knows that it is bound in the strictest sense by the words of Jesus, "You have one teacher, and you are all brothers" (Matt. 23:8). The community of faith does not need brilliant personalities but faithful servants of Jesus and of one another. It does not lack the former, but the latter. The community of faith will place its confidence only in the simple servant of the Word of Jesus, because it knows that it will then be guided not by human wisdom and human conceit, but by the Word of the Good Shepherd. The question of spiritual trust, which is so closely connected with the question of authority, is decided by the faithfulness with which people serve Jesus Christ, never by the extraordinary gifts they possess. Authority in pastoral care can be found only in the servants of Jesus who seek no authority of their own, but who are Christians one to another, obedient to the authority of the Word.

—from *Life Together* 106–107

Praying the Psalms

The Psalter is the prayer book of Jesus Christ in the truest sense of the word. He prayed the Psalter, and now it has become his prayer for all time. Can we now comprehend how the Psalter is capable of being simultaneously prayer to God and yet God's own Word, precisely because the praying Christ encounters us here? Jesus Christ prays the Psalter in his congregation. His congregation prays too, and even the individual prays. But they pray only insofar as Christ prays within them; they pray here not in their own name, but in the name of Jesus Christ. They pray not from the natural desires of their own hearts, but rather out of the humanity assumed by Christ. They pray on the basis of the prayer of the human Jesus Christ. Their prayer will be met with the promise of being heard only when they pray on this basis. Because Christ prays the prayer of the Psalms with the individual and with the church before the heavenly throne of God, or rather, because those who pray the Psalms are joining in the prayer of Jesus Christ, their prayer reaches the ears of God. Christ has become their intercessor.

—from *Life Together* 54–55

Prayers for the Community

The Psalter is the vicarious prayer of Christ for his congregation. Now that Christ is with the Father, the new humanity of Christ—the body of Christ—on earth continues to pray his prayer to the end of time. This prayer belongs not to the individual member, but to the whole body of Christ. All the things of which the Psalter speaks, which individuals can never fully comprehend and call their own, live only in the whole Christ. That is why the prayer of the Psalms belongs in the community in a special way. Even if a verse or a psalm is not my own prayer, it is nevertheless the prayer of another member of the community; and it is quite certainly the prayer of the truly human Jesus Christ and his body on earth.

—from *Life Together* 55

The School of Prayer

The Psalter is the great school of prayer. *First,* we learn here what prayer means: it means praying on the basis of the Word of God, on the basis of promises. Christian prayer takes its stand on the solid ground of the revealed Word and has nothing to do with vague, self-seeking desires. We pray on the basis of the prayer of the truly human Jesus Christ. This is what the Scripture means when it says that the Holy Spirit prays in us and for us, that Christ prays for us, that we can pray to God in the right way only in the name of Jesus Christ. *Second,* we learn from the prayer of the Psalms what we should pray. As certain as it is that the prayer of the Psalms ranges far beyond the experiences of the individual, nevertheless, the individual prays in faith the whole prayer of Christ, the prayer of one who was truly human and who alone possesses the full range of experiences expressed in these prayers.

—from *Life Together* 55–56

Prayers of Suffering

We can and we should pray the psalms of suffering, not to become completely caught up in something our heart does not know from its own experience, nor to make our own complaints, but because all this suffering was genuine and real in Jesus Christ, because the human being Jesus Christ suffered sickness, pain, shame, and death, and because in his suffering and dying all flesh suffered and died. What happened to us on the cross of Christ, the death of our old self, and what actually does happen and should happen to us since our baptism in the dying of our flesh, is what gives us the right to pray these prayers. Through the cross of Jesus these psalms have been granted to his body on earth as prayers that issue from his heart.

—from *Life Together* 56–57

Community Prayer

The prayer of the Psalms teaches us to pray as a community. The body of Christ is praying, and I as an individual recognize that my prayer is only a tiny fraction of the whole prayer of the church. I learn to join the body of Christ in its prayer. That lifts me above my personal concerns and allows me to pray selflessly. Many of the Psalms were very probably prayed antiphonally by the Old Testament congregation. The so-called parallelism of the verses, that remarkable repetition of the same idea in different words in the second line of the verse, is not merely a literary form. It also has meaning for the church and theology. . . . One might read, as a particularly clear example, Psalm 5. Repeatedly there are two voices, bringing the same prayer request to God in different words. Is that not meant to be an indication that the one who prays never prays alone? There must always be a second person, another, a member of the church, the body of Christ, indeed Jesus Christ himself, praying with the Christian in order that the prayer of the individual may be true prayer.

—from *Life Together* 57

The Law of Forgiveness

While it is true that only the sufferings of Christ are a means of atonement, yet since he has suffered for and borne the sins of the whole world and shares with his disciples the fruits of his passion, the Christian also has to undergo temptation; we too have to bear the sins of others; we too must bear their shame and be driven like a scapegoat from the gate of the city. But we would certainly break down under this burden, but for the support of him who bore the sins of all. The passion of Christ strengthens us to overcome the sins of others by forgiving them. He becomes the bearer of other person's burdens—"Bear one another's burdens, and so fulfill the law of Christ" (Gal. 6:2). As Christ bears our burdens, so ought we bear the burdens of our fellow men and women. The law of Christ, which it is our duty to fulfill, is the bearing of the cross. The burden of my brother and sister which I must bear is not only their outward lot, their natural characteristics and gifts, but quite literally their sin. And the only way to bear that sin is by forgiving it in the power of the cross of Christ in which I now share. Thus the call to follow Christ always means a call to share the work of forgiving others their sins. Forgiveness is the Christlike suffering which it is the Christian's duty to bear.

—from *A Testament to Freedom* 314

The Badge of Discipleship

Suffering, then, is the badge of true discipleship. The disciples are not above their master. Following Christ means *passio passiva*, suffering because we have to suffer. That is why Luther reckoned suffering among the marks of the true church, and one of the memoranda drawn up in preparation for the Augsburg Confession similarly defines the church as the community of those "who are persecuted and martyred for the gospel's sake." If we refuse to take up our cross and submit to suffering and rejection at human hands, we forfeit our community with Christ and have ceased to follow him. But if we lose our lives in his service and carry our cross, we shall find our lives again in the community of the cross with Christ. The opposite of discipleship is to be ashamed of Christ and his cross and all the offense which the cross brings in its train.

—from *A Testament to Freedom* 314

Surviving Suffering

Discipleship means allegiance to the suffering Christ, and it is therefore not at all surprising that Christians should be called upon to suffer. In fact it is a joy and a token of his grace. The acts of the early Christian martyrs are full of evidence which shows how Christ transfigures for his own the hour of their mortal agony by granting them the unspeakable assurance of his presence. In the hour of the cruelest torture they bear for his sake, they are made partakers in the perfect joy and bliss of fellowship with him. To bear the cross proves to be the only way of triumphing over suffering.

—from *A Testament to Freedom* 314–315

The Yoke of Christ

God is a God who *bears*. The Son of God bore our flesh, he bore the cross, he bore our sins, thus making atonement for us. In the same way his followers are also called upon to bear, and that is precisely what it means to be a Christian. Just as Christ maintained his communion with the Father by his endurance, so his followers are to maintain their communion with Christ by their endurance. We can of course shake off the burden which is laid upon us, but only find that we have a still heavier burden to carry—a yoke of our own choosing, the yoke of our self. But Jesus invites all who travail and are heavy laden to throw off their own yoke and take his yoke upon them—and his yoke is easy, and his burden is light. The yoke and the burden of Chris are his cross. To go one's way under the sign of the cross is not misery and desperation but peace and refreshment for the soul, it is the highest joy. Then we do not walk under our self-made laws and burdens, but under the yoke of him who knows us and who walks under the yoke with us. Under his yoke we are certain of his nearness and communion. It is he whom the disciple finds as he lifts up his cross.

—from *A Testament to Freedom* 315

Forgiveness without End

What path brings us to a heartfelt forgiveness of one another for every sin? Dear brothers and sisters, those who have the experience of God tearing them out of great sin and forgiving them; those to whom God has sent a brother or sister in such an hour to whom we could tell our sins; those who know the struggle the sinner wages against this help because we do not want to let ourselves be helped; and whoever nevertheless has discovered that our brother has absolved us from our sins in the name of God and in prayer—from such a one, all passion for judging and bearing grudges disappears; we want only one more thing: to share in the plight of our brother and sister, to serve, to help, to forgive, without measure, without conditions, without end. We can hate our sinful brother and sister no longer, but love them all the more, and forgive them everything, everything. O Lord, our God, let us experience your mercy, that we may practice mercy without end! Amen. Amen.

—from *A Testament to Freedom* 262–263

Free for Each Other

"The truth shall set you free" (John 8:32). Not our deed, not our courage or strength, not our people, not our truth, but God's truth alone. Why? Because to be *free* does not mean to be *great* in the world, to be free *against* our brothers and sisters, to be free *against* God; but it means to be free from ourselves, from our untruth, in which it seems as if I alone were there, as if I were the center of the world; to be free from the hatred with which I destroy God's creation; to be free from myself in order to be free for others. God's truth alone allows me to see others. It directs my attention, bent in on myself, to what is beyond and shows me the other person. And, as it does this, I experience the love and the grace of God. It destroys our untruth and creates truth. It destroys hatred and creates love. God's truth is God's love, and God's love frees us from ourselves to be free for others. To be free means nothing else than to be in this love, and to be in this love means nothing else than to be in God's truth.

—from *A Testament to Freedom* 206

Ties That Bind

It is remarkable how we think at such times about the people that we should not like to live without, and almost or entirely forget about ourselves. It is only then that we feel how closely our own lives are bound up with other people's, and in fact how the center of our own lives is outside ourselves, and how little we are separate entities. . . . I think it is a literal fact of nature that human life extends far beyond our physical existence. Probably a mother feels this more strongly than anyone else. There are two passages in the Bible which always seem to me to sum the thing up. One is from Jeremiah 45: "Behold, what I have built I am breaking down, and what I have planted I am plucking up . . . And do you seek great things for yourself? Seek them not . . . but I will give you life as a prize of war . . . ." The other is from Psalm 60: "Thou hast made the land to quake, thou hast rent it open; repair its breaches, for it totters."

—from *Letters and Papers from Prison* 45

The Wish Dream

On innumerable occasions a whole Christian community has been shattered because it has lived on the basis of a wishful image. Certainly serious Christians who are put in a community for the first time will often bring with them a very definite image of what Christian communal life should be, and they will be anxious to realize it. But God's grace quickly frustrates all such dreams. A great disillusionment with others, with Christians in general, and, if we are fortunate, with ourselves, is bound to overwhelm us as surely as God desires to lead us to an understanding of genuine Christian community. By sheer grace God will not permit us to live in a dream world even for a few weeks and to abandon ourselves to those blissful experiences and exalted moods that sweep over us like a wave of rapture. For God is not a God of emotionalism, but the God of truth. Only that community which enters into the experience of this great disillusionment with all its unpleasant and evil appearances begins to be what it should be in God's sight, begins to grasp in faith the promise that is given to it.

—from *Life Together* 35

Losing the Dream

A community that cannot bear and cannot survive . . . disillusion-ment, clinging instead to its idealized image, when that should be done away with, loses at the same time the promise of a durable Christian community. Sooner or later it is bound to collapse. Every human idealized image that is brought into the Christian community is a hindrance to genuine community and must be broken up so that genuine community can survive. Those who love their dream of a Christian community more that the Chris-tian community itself become destroyers of that Christian com-munity even though their personal intentions may be ever so honest, earnest, and sacrificial. God hates this wishful dreaming because it makes the dreamer proud and pretentious. Those who dream of this idealized community demand that it be fulfilled by God, by others, and by themselves. They enter the community of Christians with their demands, set up their own law, and judge one another and even God accordingly. They stand adamant, a liv-ing reproach to all others in the Christian community, as if their visionary ideal binds the people together. Whatever does not go their way, they call a failure. When their idealized image is shat-tered, they see the community breaking to pieces. So they first become accusers of other Christians in the community, then accusers of God, and finally the desperate accusers of themselves.

—from *Life Together* 35–36

The Gift of Community

Because God already has laid the only foundation of our community, because God has united us in one body with other Christians in Jesus Christ long before we entered into common life with them, we enter into that life together with other Christians, not as those who make demands, but as those who thankfully receive. We thank God for what God has done for us. We thank God for giving us other Christians who live by God's call, forgiveness, and promise. We do not complain about what God does not give us; rather we are thankful for what God does give us daily. And is not what has been given enough: other believers who will go on living with us through sin and need under the blessing of God's grace? Is the gift of God any less immeasurably great than this on any given day, even on the most difficult and distressing days of a Christian community?

—from *Life Together* 36

Living by the Word

Even when sin and misunderstanding burden the common life, is not the one who sins still a person with whom I too stand under the word of Christ? Will not another Christian's sin be an occasion for me ever anew to give thanks that both of us may live in the forgiving love of God in Jesus Christ? Therefore, will not the very moment of great disillusionment with my brother or sister be incomparably wholesome for me because it so thoroughly teaches me that both of us can never live by our words and deeds, but only by that one Word and deed that really binds us together, the forgiveness of sins in Jesus Christ? The bright day of Christian community dawns wherever the early morning mists of dreamy vision are lifting.

—from *Life Together* 36–37

A Little Thankfulness

Thankfulness works in the Christian community as it usually does in the Christian life. Only those who give thanks for the little things receive the great things as well. We prevent God from giving us the great spiritual gifts prepared for us because we do not give thanks for daily gifts. We think that we should to be satisfied with the small measure of spiritual knowledge, experience, and love that has been given to us, and that we must be constantly seeking the great gifts. Then we complain that we lack the deep certainty, the strong faith, and the rich experiences that God has given to other Christians, and we consider these complaints to be pious. . . . If we do not give thanks daily for the Christian community in which we have been placed, even when there are no great experiences, no noticeable riches, but much weakness, difficulty, and little faith . . . then we hinder God from letting our community grow according to the measure and riches that are there for us all in Jesus Christ.

—from *Life Together* 37

The Reality of Community

Like the Christian's sanctification, Christian community is a gift of God to which we have no claim. Only God knows the real condition of either our community or our sanctification. What may appear weak and insignificant to us may be great and glorious to God. Just as Christians should not be constantly feeling the pulse of their spiritual life, so too the Christian community has not been given to us by God for us to be continually taking its temperature. The more thankfully we daily receive what is given to us, the more assuredly and consistently will community increase and grow from day to day as God pleases. Christian community is not an ideal we have to realize, but rather a reality created by God in Christ in which we may participate. The more clearly we learn to recognize that the ground and strength and promise of all our community is in Jesus Christ alone, the more calmly we will learn to think about our community and pray and hope for it.

—from *Life Together* 38

The One Great Hope

Blessed are you outcasts and despised, you casualties of society, you men and women without work, you broken and ruined ones, you lonely and forsaken, you who endure violence and unjustly suffer, you who suffer in body and soul. Blessed are you since God's joy will come over you and will remain eternally with you. That is the gospel of the dawn of the new world, the new order, that is the world of God and the order of God. The deaf hear, the blind see, the lame walk, and the gospel is preached to the poor. . . . So seriously does God take suffering that God must immediately destroy it. The power of the demons must be broken wherever Christ is—for that reason he healed and for that reason he said to his disciples: "If you have faith, you will do greater works than I." The kingdom of God is still in the dawning. The deeds of healing are like summer lightnings, flashes out of the new world—but now the glad tidings [were] so much more powerful. Blessed are you who weep since you shall laugh, you who hunger since you will be satisfied. No cynical consolation, but it is the one great hope, the new world, the joyous tidings, the merciful God!

—from *A Testament to Freedom* 205

Thoughts on Marriage

Marriage is more than your love for each other. It has a higher dignity and power, for it is God's holy ordinance, through which God wills to perpetuate the human race till the end of time. In your love you see only your two selves in the world, but in marriage you are a link in the chain of the generations, which God causes to come and to pass away to God's glory, and calls into the kingdom. In your love you see only the heaven of your happiness, but in marriage you are placed at a post of responsibility toward the world and humanity. Your love is your own private possession, but marriage is more than something personal—it is a status, an office. Just as it is the crown, and not merely the will to rule, that makes the king, so it is marriage, and not merely your love for each other, that joins you together in the sight of God and humanity. As you first gave the ring to one another and have now received it a second time from the hand of the pastor, so love comes from you, but marriage from above, from God. As high as God is above humanity, so high are the sanctity, the rights, and the promise of marriage above the sanctity, the rights, and the promise of love. It is not your love that sustains the marriage, but from now on, the marriage that sustains your love.

—from *Letters and Papers from Prison* 27–28

Marriage for God

"Welcome one another, therefore, as Christ has welcomed you, for the glory of God" (Rom. 15:7). In a word, live together in the forgiveness of your sins, for without it no human fellowship, least of all a marriage, can survive. Don't insist on your rights, don't blame each other, don't judge or condemn each other, don't find fault with each other, but accept each other as you are, and forgive each other every day from the bottom of your hearts. From the first day of your wedding till the last the rule must be: "Welcome one another . . . for the glory of God." That is God's word for your marriage. Thank God for it; thank God for leading you thus far; ask God to establish your marriage, to confirm it, sanctify it, and preserve it. So your marriage will be "for the praise of God's glory." Amen.

—from *Letters and Papers from Prison* 31–32

Detachment

I hope that, in spite of the alerts, you are enjoying to the full the peace and beauty of these warm, summerlike Whitsuntide days. One gradually learns to acquire an inner detachment from life's menaces—although "acquire detachment" seems too negative, formal, artificial, and stoical; and it's perhaps more accurate to say that we assimilate these menaces into our life as a whole. I notice repeatedly here how few people there are who can harbor conflicting emotions at the same time. When bombers come, they are all fears; when there is something nice to eat, they are all greed; when they are disappointed, they are all despair; when they are successful, they can think of nothing else. They miss the fullness of life and the wholeness of an independent existence: everything objective and subjective is dissolved for them into fragments. By contrast, Christianity puts us into many different dimensions of life at the same time; we make room in ourselves, to some extent, for God and the whole world.

—from *A Testament to Freedom* 505

The Dimensions of Life

We rejoice with those who rejoice, and weep with those who weep; we are anxious (—I was again interrupted just then by an alert, and am now sitting out of doors enjoying the sun—) about our life, but at the same time we must think about things much more important to us than life itself. When the alert goes, for instance: as soon as we turn our minds from worrying about our own safety to the task of helping other people to keep calm, the situation is completely changed; life isn't pushed back into a single dimension, but is kept multidimensional and polyphonous. What a deliverance it is to be able to think, and thereby remain multi-dimensional. I've almost made it a rule here, simply to tell people who are trembling under an air raid that it would be much worse for a small town. We have to get people out of their one-track minds; that is a kind of "preparation" for faith, or something that makes faith possible, although really it's only faith itself that can make possible a multidimensional life, and so enable us to keep this Whitsuntide, too, in spite of the alarms.

—from *A Testament to Freedom* 506

June

The Shocking Language of Jesus

It is not for us to prophesy the day (though the day will come) when men and women will once more be called on to utter the word of God that the world will be changed and renewed by it. It will be a new language, perhaps quite nonreligious, but liberating and redeeming—as was Jesus's language; it will shock people and yet overcome them by its power; it will be the language of a new righteousness and truth, proclaiming God's peace with humanity and the coming of the kingdom. "They shall fear and tremble because of all the good and all the prosperity I provide for it" (Jer. 3:9). Till then the Christian cause will be a silent and hidden affair, but there will be those who pray and do right and wait for God's own time. May you be one of them, and may it be said of you one day, "The path of the righteous is like the light of dawn, which shines brighter and brighter till full day" (Prov. 4:18).

—from *Letters and Papers from Prison* 161–162

The Value of Friendship

There is hardly anything that can make one happier than to feel that one counts for something with other people. What matters here is not numbers, but intensity. In the long run, human relationships are the most important thing in life; the modern "efficient" person can do nothing to change this, nor can the demigods and lunatics who know nothing about human relationships. God uses us in dealing with others. Everything else is very close to hubris. Of course, one can cultivate human relationships all too consciously in an attempt to mean something to other people, as I have been realizing lately in the letters of Gabriele von Bülow-Humboldt; it may lead to an unrealistic cult of the human. I mean, in contrast to that, that people are more important than anything else in life. That certainly does not mean undervaluing the world of things and practical efficiency. But what is the finest book, or picture, or house, or estate, to me, compared to my wife, my parents, or my friend?

—from *Letters and Papers from Prison* 205

Love One Another

What does it mean to be a Christian congregation when in the midst of many beneficial and nice activities that may take place in it, the one thing needful is not completely clear or obvious—that the members of the congregation are simply to love one another? What kind of picture does a church offer itself and the world when not even this foremost duty is taken seriously? If anything human in the early church was able to convince the pagans it was simply this—they could see, really see with their very eyes, that the two neighbors, the master and his slaves, the brothers on bad terms with each other all at once were no longer against each other, but with each other and for each other. When they became Christians, they simply experienced radical outward changes. Do we think perhaps that because we are already Christians, nothing needs to change anymore? Or hadn't we better say: If we would really become Christians, immediately much would change in our lives too? Do not these words bring judgment even to a Christian community even if everything as happening in a congregation, even if they all came to church, even if they did many good things and yet "if it has not love, it is nothing."

—from *A Testament to Freedom* 239

Life and Love

A life has meaning and value only in so far as love is in it. Furthermore, life is nothing, nothing at all, and has not meaning and value if love is not in it. The worth of a life is measured by how much love it has. Everything else is nothing, nothing at all, totally indifferent, totally unimportant. All the bad things and all the good things about life, all the large and small matters of life are unimportant. We are only asked about one thing—whether we have love or not. . . . Life is really not worth living at all without love. However, the whole meaning of life is fulfilled where there is love. In comparison to this love everything else pales into insignificance. What do happiness and unhappiness mean, what do wealth and poverty mean, what do honor and disgrace mean, what does living at home or abroad mean, what does life and death mean where people live in love? They do not know. They do not differentiate. They only know that the sole purpose of happiness as well as unhappiness, poverty as well as wealth, honor as well as disgrace, living at home or abroad, living and dying is to love all the more strongly, purely, fully. It is the one thing beyond all distinctions, before all distinctions, in all distinctions. "Love is as strong as death" (Song of Songs 8:6).

—from *A Testament to Freedom* 241

JUNE 5

The Upside-Down World

If the final "condemned" or "saved" that is to be spoken over our life really only depends on whether a person had love or not; if the verdict before God's throne actually needs "love or nothing," then all of a sudden the world looks very different than before, then all of a sudden much of what was previously big in the world abruptly plunges down into this nothingness, this emptiness, this destruction of life. Whoever strived for power and authority and honor, for pleasure and material wealth, whoever elevated oneself up above this world is toppled, judged, destroyed by this simple word of the New Testament (see 1 Cor. 13:1–3). This striving is nothing, nothing at all. The world order is turned upside down when it takes these words seriously: "but [if I] have not love, I am nothing." But what really matters now is that our piety, our Christianity, our religious life, and all its seriousness has also fallen along with the world. . . . In the presence of love, everything else becomes small.

—from *A Testament to Freedom* 241–242

171

Misguided Love

It is true that there is not one who lives without love. Each individual has love. We know about its power and its passion. We even know that this love makes up the whole meaning of our life. We would be tempted to throw away our whole life if it did not have this love we have experienced because it would no longer be worth living. Everyone knows about the power, passion, and meaning of this love. However, this love is our love of ourselves. It is this love that fulfills us and makes us enterprising and resourceful. . . . This is the way we experience love, but only in its diabolical reflections and caricature as self-love. However this self-love is misguided love that has rebelled against its source, love that does not need the help of others and thus is condemned to be unfruitful, love that is basically enmity toward God and one's neighbor because they could only disturb the immediate circle of myself. Both types of love actually have the same power, the same passion, the same exclusivity. The only thing that sets them apart is the tremendously different goal they each have—in one case, I myself, in the other, God and my neighbor.

—from *A Testament to Freedom* 245–246

The Love of the Cross

Those who believe all things and hope all things for the sake of love, for the sake of encouraging and helping others must suffer and endure. For the world takes them for fools, perhaps even for dangerous fools because their foolishness may even provoke malice into exposing itself. But only when malice comes to light can it ever be fully loved. Therefore love endures all things and is radiant and happy in this suffering. For this suffering and endurance make love greater and greater and more and more irresistible. Love that endures all things gains the victory. Who is this love if not the one who bore all things, believed all things, hoped all things, and even had to endure all things all the way to the cross? The one who did not insist on his own way nor seek himself, the one who did not allow himself to become bitter, and who did not keep a record of the evil deeds perpetrated on him and thus was overwhelmed by evil? The one who even prayed on the cross for his enemies and in this act of love utterly overcame evil. Who is this love Paul spoke of in these verses if not Jesus Christ himself? Who is meant here if not Jesus? What is the mark of the whole chapter [of 1 Corinthians 13] if not the cross.

—from *A Testament to Freedom* 247–248

The Loving Church

A church of faith—even if it is the most orthodox faith that faithfully adheres to the creeds—is of no use if it is not even more a
church of pure and all-embracing love. What does it mean to
believe in Christ who was love and still be full of hatred yourself?
What does it meant to call Christ one's Lord in faith and not to
do his will? Such faith is not faith at all, but hypocrisy. It is of no
use to us for us to confess our faith in Christ if we have not gone
first and reconciled ourselves to our brothers and sisters, even to
the godless, racially different, ostracized, and outcast. And a church
that calls a nation to faith in Christ must itself be the burning fire
of love in this nation, the driving force for reconciliation, the place
in which all the fires of hatred are extinguished and prideful, hate-
filled people are turned into people who love. Our Reformation
churches have accomplished great things, and yet it seems to me
that they have not yet succeeded in doing this greatest of all
things. Today it is more necessary than ever.

—from *A Testament to Freedom* 249

Hope beyond Measure

A faith that really keeps to what is invisible and lives by it, acting as if it were already here, hopes at the same time for the time of fulfillment, of seeing and possessing. We hope for it as confidently as the hungry child to whom his father has promised bread can wait a while because he believes. Yet eventually the child wants to get the bread. Or take the music listener who willingly follows a dark interplay of disharmonies, but only in the certainty that these disharmonies will have to be resolved sooner or later. Or think of the patient who takes a bitter medicine so that the pain is finally taken away. A faith that does not hope is sick. It is like a hungry child who does not want to eat or a tired person who does not want to sleep. Humankind hopes as surely as it believes. And it is not a disgrace to hope even beyond measure.

—from *A Testament to Freedom* 250

Hope Remains

Who would even want to speak of God without hoping to see God one day? Who would want to talk about peace or love among people without wanting to experience them one day in eternity? Who would want to talk about a new world and a new humanity without hoping that we would share in it? And why should we be ashamed of our hope? One day we will have to be ashamed not of our hope but of our pitiful and fearful hopelessness which believes God is capable of very little, and in false humility does not act where God's promises are given. Such hopelessness gives up in this life and is not capable of looking forward to God's eternal power and glory. . . . "Hope does not disappoint us" (Rom. 5:5). The more a person dares to hope, the greater that person becomes with God's hope. People grow with their hope, if only it is hope in God and God's power alone. Hope remains.

—from *A Testament to Freedom* 250–251

Faith, Hope, and Love

What could be greater than to live one's life in faith before God? What could be greater than to live one's life to God in hope? Even greater is the love which lives *in* God. "Walk before me" (Gen. 17:1). "Whoever lives in love lives *in God* (1 John 4:10). What is greater than the humility of faith which never forgets the infinite distance of the Creator from the creature? What is greater than the confidence of hope which longs for God's coming and longs to see God's reality? Even greater is love, for already here it is certain of God's nearness and presence everywhere. This love clings to God's love and knows that God's love wants nothing but our love. What is greater than faith which hopes for its salvation in Christ and holds fast to Christ and is justified in him? What is greater than hope which hour after hour focuses on a blessed experience of dying and a radiant homecoming? Even greater is the love that senses, the love that forgets everything for the other and even sacrifices one's own salvation to bring it to one's family. For "whoever loses his life for my sake will find if" (Matt. 16:25). Faith and hope remain. Let us not think that we can have love without faith and without hope! Love without faith is like a river without a source. That would mean we could have love without Christ. Faith alone justifies us before God. Hope directs our attention to the end. Love perfects.

—from *A Testament to Freedom* 251

The Church in the World

Christ is present in his church today. This church is no ideal church, but a reality in the world, a bit of the world reality. The secularity of the church follows from the incarnation of Christ. The church, like Christ, has become world. It is a denial of the real humanity of Jesus and also heretical to take the concrete church as only a phantom church or an illusion. It is entirely world. This means that it is subjected to all the weakness and suffering of the world. The church can at times, like Christ himself, be without a roof over its head. This must be so. For the sake of real people, the church must be thoroughly worldly. It is a worldly reality for our sakes. Real secularity consists in the church's being able to renounce all privileges and all its property but never Christ's Word and the forgiveness of sins. With Christ and the forgiveness of sins to fall back on, the church is free to give up everything else.

—from *A Testament to Freedom* 86–87

The Judgment of the Church

While the church is in the world and is even a bit of the world, it cannot hope to represent itself as a visible communion of saints. Secularity means renunciation of the ideal of purity. This has nothing to do with secularization. The church has been in process of becoming world, not some "pure" entity, since its origins. Not even primitive Christianity was "pure." Otherwise, one confuses church with a religious community and the gospel with the ideal of an experience. Perfectionistic sectarianism from Greek mysticism to Tolstoy has attempted to usurp the Kingdom of God for itself (Matt. 11:12). They pretend to have revealed this kingdom. They pretend to have made it clearly visible in the holiness of people. However, the church, having become the worldly form or revelation, ought not to succumb to this temptation. It ought not to seek to justify itself before itself and before the world. Its justification comes from God alone. It cannot anticipate the last judgment. "You shall not judge!" also applies here. God has reserved to the divine self the separation of the wheat from the chaff.

—from *A Testament to Freedom* 87

A Communion of Sinners

The church . . . remains the church of the baptized and, therefore, a communion of sinners. All baptized persons belong to it, no matter what their works may seem to be. Renunciation of its claims to "purity" leads the church back to its solidarity with the sinful world. Through courageous acknowledgment of its being world, the church is perfectly free from the world to become Christian. It has no more respect for the "shrines" of the world. Face to face with outcasts, it is as free as the nobility. It has as its place not only with the poor but also with the rich; not only with the pious, but also with the Godless. All are world. It faces both groups with the same impartiality. There is no sphere from which it distances itself out of anxiety over going astray. Faith has completely conquered the world both for the outcast and for the rich. Only this kind of church is wholly free, the church that confesses its secularity and thereby claims to be an *ecclesia perfecta,* or perfect church.

—from *A Testament to Freedom* 87

The Otherworldly Church

We are otherworldly—ever since we hit upon the devious trick of being religious, yes even "Christian," at the expense of the earth. Otherworldliness affords a splendid environment in which to live. Whenever life begins to become oppressive and troublesome we just leap into the air with a bold kick and soar relieved and unencumbered into so-called eternal fields. We leap over the present. We distain the earth; we are better than it. After all, besides the temporal defeats we still have our eternal victories, and they are so easily achieved. Otherworldliness also makes it easy to preach and to speak words of comfort. An otherworldly church can be certain that it will in no time win over all the weaklings, all who are only too glad to be deceived and deluded, all utopianists, all disloyal children of the earth. When an explosion seems imminent, who would not be so human as to quickly mount the chariot that comes down from the skies with the promise of taking us to a better world beyond . . . ? We are weak; we cannot bear having the earth so near, the earth that bears us. We cannot stand it, because the earth is stronger than we and because we want to be better than the evil earth. So we extricate ourselves from it; we refuse to take it seriously. . . . However, Christ does not will or intend this weakness; instead, he makes us strong. He does not lead us in a religious flight from this world to other worlds beyond; rather, he gives us back to the earth as its loyal children.

—from *A Testament to Freedom* 89

The Day's Refreshment

The breaking of bread has a festive quality. In the midst of the working day given to us again and again, it is a reminder that God rested after God's work, and that the Sabbath is the meaning and the goal of the week with its toil. Our life is not only a great deal of trouble and hard work; it is also refreshment and joy in God's goodness. We labor, but God nourishes and sustains us. That is a reason to celebrate. People should not eat the bread of anxious toil (Ps. 127:2). Rather "eat your bread with enjoyment" (Eccl. 9:7), "so I commend enjoyment, for there is nothing better for people under the sun than to eat, and drink, and enjoy themselves" (Eccl. 8:15). But of course, "apart from him, who can eat or who can have enjoyment?" (Eccl. 2:25). It is said of the seventy elders of Israel who climbed Mount Sinai with Moses and Aaron that "they beheld God, and they ate and drank" (Exodus 24:11). God will not tolerate the unfestive, joyless manner in which we eat our bread with sighs of groaning, with pompous, self-important busyness, or even with shame. Through the daily meal God is calling us to rejoice, to celebrate in the midst of our working day.

—from *Life Together* 73

The Church Renewed

Reconciliation and redemption, regeneration and the Holy Ghost, love of our enemies, cross and resurrection, life in Christ and Christian discipleship—all these things are so difficult and so remote that we hardly venture anymore to speak of them. In the traditional words and acts we suspect that there may be something quite new and revolutionary, though we cannot as yet grasp or express it. That is our own fault. Our Church, which has been fighting in these years only for its self-preservation, as though that were an end in itself, is incapable of taking the word of reconciliation and redemption to mankind and the world. Our earlier words are therefore bound to lose their force and cease, and our being Christians today will be limited to two things: prayer and righteous action among humanity. All Christian thinking, speaking, and organizing must be born anew out of this prayer and action.

—from *Letters and Papers from Prison* 161

There Shall Be Peace

There shall be peace because of the church of Christ, for the sake of whom the world exists. And this church of Christ lives at one and the same time in all peoples, yet beyond all boundaries, whether national, political, social, or racial. And the Christians who make up this church are bound together, through the commandment of the one Lord Christ, whose Word they hear, more inseparably than people are bound by all the ties of the common history, of blood, of class, and of language. All these ties, which are part of our world, are valid ties, not indifferent; but in the presence of Christ they are not ultimate bonds. For the members of the ecumenical church, insofar as they hold to Christ, his word, his commandment of peace, is more holy, more inviolable than the most revered words and works of the natural world. For they know that whoso are not able to hate father and mother for his sake are not worthy of him, and lie if they call themselves after Christ's name. These brothers and sisters in Christ obey his word; they do not doubt or question, but keep his commandment of peace. They are not ashamed, in defiance of the world, even to speak of eternal peace. They cannot take up arms against Christ himself—yet this is what they do if they take up arms against one another! Even in anguish and distress of conscience there is for them no escape from the commandment of Christ that there shall be peace.

—from *A Testament to Freedom* 228

The Way to Peace

How does peace come about? Through a system of political treaties? Through the investment of international capital in different countries? Through the big banks, through money? Or through universal peaceful rearmament in order to guarantee peace? Through none of these, for the single reason that in all of them peace is confused with safety. There is no way to peace along the way of safety. For peace must be dared. It is the great venture. It can never be safe. Peace is the opposite of security. To demand guarantees is to want to protect oneself. Peace means to give oneself altogether to the law of God, wanting no security, but in faith and obedience laying the destiny of the nations in the hand of the Almighty God, not trying to direct it for selfish purposes. Battles are won, not with weapons, but with God. They are won where the way leads to the cross. Which of us can say he or she knows what it might mean for the world if one nation should meet the aggressor, not with weapons in hand, but praying, defenseless, and for that very reason protected by "a bulwark never failing."

—from *A Testament to Freedom* 228

Sing a New Song

"O sing to the Lord a new song," the Psalter calls out to us again and again. It is the Christ hymn, new every morning, that a community living together begins to sing. . . . Every day in the morning the community of faith on earth joins in this song and in the evening it closes the day with this hymn. The triune God and the works of God are being extolled here. This song has a different sound on earth than it does in heaven. On earth, it is the song of those who believe; in heaven, the song of those who see. On earth, it is a song expressed in inadequate human words; in heaven they are the "things that are not to be told, that no mortal is permitted to repeat" (2 Cor. 12:4), the "new song that no one could learn, except the 144,000" (Rev. 14:3), the song to which the "harps of God" are played (Rev. 15:2). . . . Our new song is an earthly song, a song of pilgrims and sojourners on whom the Word of God has dawned to light their way. Our earthly song is bound to God's Word of revelation in Jesus Christ. It is the simple song of the children of this earth who have been called to be God's children, not ecstatic, not enraptured, but soberly, gratefully, devoutly focused on God's revealed Word.

—from *Life Together* 65–66

Singing in Unity

Why do Christians sing when they are together? The reason is, quite simply, that in singing together it is possible for them to speak and pray the same Word at the same time—in other words, for the sake of uniting in the Word. All daily worship, all human concentration should be focused on the Word in the hymn. The fact that we do not speak it in unison, but sing it, only expresses the fact that our spoken words are inadequate to express what we want to say, that the object of our singing reaches far beyond all human words. Nevertheless, we do not mumble unintelligible words; rather we sing words of praise to God, words of thanksgiving, confession, and prayer. Thus the music is completely the servant of the Word. It elucidates the Word in its incomprehensibility. . . . Here words and music combine in a unique way. The freely soaring tone of unison singing finds its sole and essential inner support in the words that are sung. . . . The essence of all congregational singing on this earth is the purity of unison singing—untouched by the unrelated motives of musical excess—the clarity unclouded by the dark desire to lend musicality an autonomy of its own apart from the words; it is the simplicity and unpretentiousness, the humanness and warmth, of this style of singing. . . . It is singing from the heart, singing to the Lord, singing the Word; this is singing in unity.

—from *Life Together* 66–67

Prayers of the People

No matter what objections there may be to prayer together, it simply could not be any other way. Christians may and should pray together to God in their own words when they desire to live together under the Word of God. They have requests, gratitude, and intercessions to bring in common to God, and they should do so joyfully and confidently. All our fear of one another, all our inhibitions about praying freely in our own words in the presence of others, can diminish where the common prayer of the community is brought before God by one of its members with dignity and simplicity. Likewise, however, all our observations and criticisms should cease whenever weak words of prayer are offered in the name of Jesus Christ. It is in fact the most normal thing in our common Christian life to pray together. As good and useful as our scruples may be about keeping our prayer pure and biblical, they must nevertheless not stifle the free prayer itself that is so necessary, for it has been endowed with great promise by Jesus Christ.

—from *Life Together* 69

The Rise of Radicalism

Radicalism always arises from a conscious or unconscious hatred of what exists. Christian radicalism, whether it would flee the world or improve it, comes from the hatred of creation. The radical cannot forgive God for having created what is. It is Ivan Karamazov, the one totally at odds with the created world, who creates the figure of a radical Jesus in the legend of the Grand Inquisitor. When evil becomes powerful in the world, it simultaneously injects the Christian with the poison of radicalism. Reconciliation with the world as it is, which is given to the Christian by Christ, is then called betrayal and denial of Christ. In its place come bitterness, suspicion, and contempt for human beings and the world. Love that believes all things, bears all things, and hopes all things, love that loves the world in its very wickedness with the love of God (John 3:16), becomes—by limiting love to the closed circle of the pious—a pharisaical refusal of love for the wicked. The open church of Jesus Christ, which serves the world to the end, becomes kind of supposed ur-Christian ideal church-community that in turn mistakenly confuses the realization of a Christian idea with the reality the living Jesus Christ. Thus a world that has become evil succeeds in making Christians evil also.

—from *Ethics* 155–156

The Sins of the Church

The church confesses that it has not professed openly and clearly enough its message of the one God, revealed for all times in Jesus Christ and tolerating no other gods besides. The church confesses its timidity, its deviations, its dangerous concessions. It has often disavowed its duties as sentinel and comforter. Through this it has often withheld the compassion that it owes to the despised and rejected. The church was mute when it should have cried out, because the blood of the innocent cried out to heaven. The church did not find the right word in the right way at the right time. It did not resist to the death the falling away from faith and is guilty of the godlessness of the masses. The church confesses that it has misused the name of Christ by being ashamed of it before the world and by not resisting strongly enough the misuse of that name for evil ends. The church has looked on while injustice and violence have been done, under the cover of the name of Christ. It has even allowed the most holy name to be openly derided without contradiction and has thus encouraged that derision. The church recognizes that God will not leave unpunished those who so misuse God's name as it does.

—from *Ethics* 138–139

The Sin of Silence

The church confesses that it has witnessed the arbitrary use of brutal force, the suffering in body and soul of countless innocent people, that it has witnessed oppression, hatred, and murder without raising its voice for the victims and without finding ways of rushing to help them. It has become guilty of the lives of the weakest and most defenseless brothers and sisters of Jesus Christ. . . . The church confesses that it has looked on silently as the poor were exploited and robbed, while the strong were enriched and corrupted. The church confesses its guilt toward the countless people whose lives have been destroyed by slander, denunciation, and defamation. It has not condemned the slanderers for their wrongs and has thereby left the slandered to their fate. The church confesses that it has coveted security, tranquility, peace, property, and honor to which it had no claim, and therefore has not bridled human covetousness, but promoted it.

—from *Ethics* 139–140

The Sin of Acquiescence

The church confesses itself guilty of violating all of the Ten Commandments. It confesses thereby its apostasy from Christ. It has not so borne witness to the truth of God in a way that leads all inquiry and science to recognize its origin in this truth. It has not so proclaimed the righteousness of God that all human justice must see there its own source and essence. It has not been able to make the loving care of God so credible that all human economic activity would be guided by it in its task. By falling silent the church became guilty for the loss of responsible action in society, courageous intervention, and the readiness to suffer for what is acknowledged as right. It is guilty of the government's falling away from Christ.

—from *Ethics* 140–141

The Necessity of Confession

Is this going too far? Should a few super-righteous people rise at this point and try to prove that not the church but all the others are guilty? Would a few churchmen like to dismiss this as a rude insult and, presuming to be called as judges of the world, proceed to weigh the mass of guilt here and there and distribute it accordingly? Was not the church hindered and bound on all sides? Was not all worldly power arrayed against it? Should the church have endangered its ultimate purpose, its public worship and its congregational life, by taking up the struggle against anti-Christian powers? So speaks unbelief, which perceives confession of guilt not as regaining the form of Jesus Christ who bore the sins of the world, but only as a dangerous moral degradation. Free confession of guilt is not something that one can take or leave; it is the form of Jesus Christ breaking through in the church. The church can let this happen to itself, or it will cease to be the church of Christ. Whoever stifles or spoils the church's confession of guilt is hopelessly guilty before Christ. In confessing its guilt the church does not release people from their personal confession of guilt, but calls everyone into a community of confession. Only as judged by Christ can humanity that has fallen away exist before Christ. The church calls all whom it reaches to come under this judgment.

—from *Ethics* 141–142

The Confession of Faith

No religious service should be without confession of faith. This differentiates the community from the general public. The community must either confess its faith or disavow it. It cannot, like the general public, remain undecided. Aesthetic hesitations do not count for much here. Confession of faith is the only genuine attitude with which the community entrusts itself. It orders its life both inwardly and outwardly through the confession of faith. Through this confession the community distinguishes itself from the world. The confession of faith must be a wholly sincere response to God's Word of truth. Confession of faith is a matter of immediate presence. It doesn't pertain to aesthetic judgment; nor is it prayed for; it can only be confessed: "I acknowledge and confess your truth, O God." The apostolic confession doesn't suffice. Confession of faith is a matter of our true, present stance before God. Here no definitive role has been granted to mere tradition. The spoken word itself and not just what is meant must be genuine in our confession of faith. For the sake of our love of the community our word ought to be clean and unequivocal.

—from *A Testament to Freedom* 85–86

Discipline of the Secret

Confession of faith is not to be confused with professing a religion. Such profession uses the confession as propaganda and ammunition against the Godless. The confession of faith belongs rather to the "Discipline of the Secret" in the Christian gathering of those who believe. Nowhere else is it tenable. . . . The primary confession of the Christian before the world is the deed which interprets itself. If this deed is to become a force, then the world itself will long to confess the Word. This is not the same as loudly shrieking out propaganda. This Word must be preserved as the most sacred possession of the community. This is a matter between God and the community, not between the community and the world. It is the word of recognition between friends, not a word to use against our enemies. This attitude was first learned at baptism. The deed alone in our confession of faith before the world.

—from *A Testament to Freedom* 86

Forgiveness without Words

We may suffer the sins of one another; we do not need to judge. That is grace for Christians. For what sin ever occurs in the community that does not lead Christians to examine themselves and condemn themselves for their own lack of faithfulness in prayer and in intercession, for their lack of service to one another in mutual admonition and comforting, indeed, for their own personal sin and lack of spiritual discipline by which they have harmed themselves, the community, and one another? Because each individual's sin burdens the whole community and indicts it, the community of faith rejoices amid all the pain inflicted on it by the sin of the other and, in spite of the burden placed on it, rejoices in being deemed worthy of bearing with and forgiving sin. . . . The service of forgiveness is done by one to the other on a daily basis. It occurs *without words* in intercessory prayer for on another. And all members of the community who do not grow tired of doing this service can depend on the fact that this service is also being offered to them by other Christians. Those who bear with others know that they themselves are being borne. Only in this strength can they themselves bear with others.

—from *A Testament to Freedom* 102–103

July

The Merciful

"Blessed are the merciful, for they will receive mercy."

These persons without possessions, these strangers on earth, these powerless people, these sinners, these followers of Jesus, have in their life with him *renounced their own dignity*, for they are compassionate. As if their own needs and their own poverty were not enough, they take upon themselves the needs and humiliation and sin of strangers. They have an irresistible love for the down-trodden, the sick, the wretched, the degraded, the oppressed, for those who suffer unjustly, for the outcast, and for all who are tortured with anxiety. They go out and seek all who are enmeshed in the toils of sin and guilt. No distress is too great, no sin too appalling for their compassion. . . . They will be found consorting with publicans and sinners, careless of the shame they incur thereby. In order that they may be compassionate they cast away the most priceless treasure of human life, their personal dignity and honor. For the only honor and dignity they know is their Lord's own mercy, to which alone they owe their very lives.

—from *A Testament to Freedom* 315–316

The Peacemakers

"Blessed are the peacemakers, for they will be called children of God."

The followers of Jesus have been called to peace. When Jesus called them, they found their peace. For Jesus is their peace. But now they are told that they must not only *have* peace but *make* it. And to that end they renounce all violence and rioting. In the cause of Christ such actions are never of any help. The kingdom of Christ is a kingdom of peace; and those in the community of Christ greet one another with the greeting of peace. The disciples of Jesus keep the peace to the extent that they themselves would rather suffer than inflict suffering on others. They preserve community where others would break it up. They renounce aggressivity on their own behalf and quietly suffer hatred and injustice. In this way they overcome evil with good and thus bring about the peace of God in the midst of a world of hatred and war. But nowhere will their peace be greater than where they encounter evil people in peace and are ready to suffer at their hands. The peacemakers will carry the cross with their Lord, for it was on the cross that peace was made. Because they are so caught up in the work of Christ for peace, because their mission is to do the work of the Son of God, therefore they are called God's own children.

—from *A Testament to Freedom* 316

The Persecuted

"Blessed are those who are persecuted for righteousness' sake,
for theirs is the kingdom of heaven."

This does not refer to the righteousness of God but to suffering for a just cause, to the suffering of the disciples of Jesus because of their just judgment and action. For it is in judgment and deed that those who follow Jesus in the renunciation of their possessions, good fortune, rights, righteousness, honor, and the resort to violence will be distinguished from the world. They will offend the world. Therefore, the followers [of Christ] will be persecuted for their righteousness. Not recognition but rejection by the world is the reward they will get for their words and actions. It is important that Jesus also declare blessed not only those who suffer directly for the confession of his name but also those who suffer for a just cause. They are made sharers in the same promise as the poor because those who suffer persecution are their equals in poverty.

—from *A Testament to Freedom* 316

Losing Freedom

My cell is being cleaned out for me, and while it is being done, I can give the cleaner something to eat. One of them was sentenced to death the other day; it gave me a great shock. One sees a great deal in seven and a half months, particularly what heavy consequences may follow trivial acts of folly. I think a lengthy confinement is demoralizing in *every* way for most people. I have been thinking out an alternative penal system on the principle of making the punishment fit the crime; e.g., for absence without leave, the canceling of leave; for the unauthorized wearing of medals, longer service at the front; for robbing other soldiers, the temporary labeling of the man as a thief; for dealing in the black market, a reduction of rations; and so on. Why does the Old Testament law never punish anyone by depriving him of his freedom?

—from *Letters and Papers from Prison* 78

The Bigger Question

What does it mean to "interpret in a religious sense"? I think it means to speak on the one hand metaphysically, and on the other hand individualistically. Neither of these is relevant to the biblical message or to people today. Hasn't the individualistic question about personal salvation almost completely left us all? Aren't we really under the impression that there are more important things than that question (perhaps not more important than the *matter* itself, but more important than the *question!*)? I know it sounds pretty monstrous to say that. But, fundamentally, isn't this in fact biblical? Does the question about saving one's soul appear in the Old Testament at all? Aren't righteousness and the kingdom of God on earth the focus of everything, and isn't it true that Romans 3:24ff is not an individualistic doctrine of salvation, but the culmination of the view that God alone is righteous? It is not with the beyond that we are concerned, but with this world as created and preserved, subjected to laws, reconciled, and restored. What is above this world is, in the gospel, intended to exist *for* this world; I mean that, not in the anthropocentric sense of the liberal, mystic, pietistic, ethical theology, but in the biblical sense of the creation and of the incarnation, crucifixion, and resurrection of Jesus Christ.

—from *A Testament to Freedom* 504

Real Suffering

When people suggest in their letters ... that I am "suffering" here, I reject the thought, for it seems to me a profanation. These things must not be dramatized. I doubt very much whether I am "suffering" any more than you, or most people, are suffering today. Of course, a great deal here is horrible, but where isn't it? Perhaps we have made too much of this question of suffering, and been too solemn about it. I have sometimes been surprised that the Roman Catholics take so little notice of that kind of thing. Is it because they are stronger than we are? Perhaps they know better from their own history what suffering and martyrdom really are, and are silent about petty inconveniences and obstacles. I believe, for instance, that physical sufferings, actual pain and so on, are certainly to be classed as "suffering." We so like to stress spiritual suffering; and yet that is just what Christ is supposed to have taken from us, and I can find nothing about it in the New Testament, or in the acts of the early martyrs. After all, whether "the Church suffers" is not at all the same as whether one of its servants has to put up with this or that. I think we need a good deal of correction on this point; indeed, I must admit candidly that I sometimes feel almost ashamed of how often we have talked about our own sufferings. No, suffering must be something quite different, and have a quite different dimension, from what I have so far experienced.

—from *Letters and Papers from Prison* 126

No Words

Those who had been bombed out came to me the next morning for a bit of comfort. But I am afraid I am bad at comforting; I can listen all right, but I can hardly ever find anything to say. But perhaps the way one asks about some things and not about others helps to suggest what really matters; and it seems to me more important actually to share someone's distress than to use smooth words about it. I have no sympathy with some wrong-headed attempts to explain away distress, because instead of being a comfort, they are the exact opposite. So I do not try to explain it, and I think that is the right way to begin, although it is only a beginning, and I very seldom get beyond it. I sometimes think that real discomfort must break in just as unexpectedly as the distress.

—from *Letters and Papers from Prison* 109

The Will of God

The question of the will of God must take the place of the question about one's own being good and doing good. But the will of God is nothing other than the realization of the Christ-reality among us and in our world. The will of God is therefore not an idea that demands to be realized; it is itself already reality in the self-revelation of God in Jesus Christ. The will of God is neither an idea nor is it simply identical with what exists, so that subjection to things as they are could fulfill it; it is rather a reality that wills to become real ever anew in what exists and against what exists. The will of God has already been fulfilled by God, in reconciling the world to himself in Christ. To disregard the reality of this fulfillment and to set a fulfillment of one's own in its place would be the most dangerous relapse into abstract thinking. Since the appearance of Christ, ethics can be concerned with only one thing: to partake in the reality of the fulfilled will of God. But to partake in this is possible only because of the fact that even I myself am already included in the fulfillment of the will of God in Christ, which means that I have been reconciled to God.

—from *Ethics* 74

Between Silence and Speech

Wherever the service of listening, active helpfulness, and bearing with others is being faithfully performed, the ultimate and highest ministry can also be offered, the service of the Word of God. This service has to do with the free word from person to person, not the word bound to a particular pastoral office, time, and place. It is a matter of that unique situation in which one person bears witness in human words to another person regarding all the comfort, the admonition, the kindness, and the firmness of God. This word is threatened all about by endless dangers. If proper listening does not precede it, how can it really be the right word for the other? If it is contradicted by one's own lack of helpfulness, how can it be a credible and truthful word? If it does not flow from the act of bearing with others, but from impatience and the spirit of violence against others, how can it be the liberating and healing word? . . . But, on the other hand, who wants to accept the responsibility for having been silent when we should have spoken? The orderly word spoken in the pulpit is so much easier than this totally free word, standing responsibly between silence and speech.

—from *Life Together* 103

The Enemy of the Church

Cheap grace is the deadly enemy of our church. We are fighting today for costly grace. Cheap grace means grace sold on the market like the cheap wares of a bargain huckster. The sacraments, the forgiveness of sin, and the consolations of religion are thrown away at cut prices. Grace is represented as the church's inexhaustible treasury, from which the church showers blessings with generous hands, without asking questions or fixing limits. Grace without price; grace without cost! The essence of grace, we suppose, is that the account has been paid in advance; and, because it has been paid, everything can be had for nothing. Since the cost was infinite, the possibilities of using and spending it are infinite. What would grace be if it were not cheap? Cheap grace means grace as a doctrine, a principle, a system. It means forgiveness of sins proclaimed as a general truth, the love of God taught as the Christian "conception" of God. An intellectual assent to that idea is held to be of itself sufficient to secure remission of sins. The church which holds the correct doctrine of grace has, it is supposed, ipso facto a part in that grace. In such a church the world finds a cheap covering for its sins; no contrition is required, still less any real desire to be delivered from sin. Cheap grace therefore amounts to a denial of the living Word of God, in fact, a denial of the Incarnation of the Word of God.

—from *A Testament to Freedom* 307–308

Cheap Grace

Cheap grace is the preaching of forgiveness without requiring repentance, baptism without church discipline, communion without confession, absolution without personal confession. Cheap grace is grace without discipleship, grace without the cross, grace without Jesus Christ, living and incarnate. Costly grace is the gospel which must be *sought* again and again, the gift which must be *asked* for, the door at which a person must *knock*. Such grace is *costly* because it calls us to follow, and it is *grace* because it calls us to follow *Jesus Christ*. It is costly because it costs us our life, and it is grace because it gives us the only true life. It is costly because it condemns sin, and grace because it justifies the sinner. Above all, it is *costly* because it cost God the life of God's Son: "you were bought at a price," and what has cost God much cannot be cheap for us. Above all, it is *grace* because God did not reckon God's Son too dear a price to pay for our life, but delivered him up for us. Costly grace is the Incarnation of God.

—from *A Testament to Freedom* 308

The Price of Grace

Costly grace is the sanctuary of God; it has to be protected from the world, and not thrown to the dogs. It is therefore the living Word, the Word of God, which God speaks as it pleases God. Costly grace confronts us as a gracious call to follow Jesus, it comes as a word of forgiveness to the broken spirit and the contrite heart. Grace is costly because it compels a person to submit to the yoke of Christ and follow him; it is grace because Jesus says: "My yoke is easy and my burden is light. . . ."

—from *A Testament to Freedom* 308

Grace for Sale

Is the price that we are paying today with the collapse of the organized churches anything else but an inevitable consequence of grace acquired too cheaply? We gave away preaching and sacraments cheaply; we performed baptisms and confirmations; we absolved an entire people, unquestioned and unconditionally; out of human love we handed over what was holy to the scornful and unbelievers. We poured out rivers of grace without end, but the call to rigorously follow Christ was seldom heard. What happened to the insights of the ancient church, which in the baptismal teaching watched so carefully over the boundary between the church and the world, over costly grace? What happened to Luther's warnings against a proclamation of the gospel which made people secure in their godless lives? When was the world ever Christianized more dreadfully and wickedly than here? What do the three thousand Saxons whose bodies Charlemagne killed compare with the millions of souls being killed today? The biblical wisdom that the sins of the fathers are visited on the children unto the third and fourth generations has become true in us. Cheap grace was very unmerciful to our Protestant church.

—from *Discipleship* 53–54

Unmerciful Grace

Cheap grace surely has also been unmerciful with most of us personally. It did not open the way to Christ for us, but rather closed it. It did not call us into discipleship, but hardened us in disobedience. Moreover, was it not unmerciful and cruel when we were accosted by the message of cheap grace just where we had once heard the call to follow Jesus as Christ's call of grace, where we perhaps had once dared to take the first steps of discipleship in the discipline of obedience to the commandments? Could we hear this message in any other way than that it tried to block our way with the call to a highly worldly sobriety which suffocated our joy in discipleship by pointing out that it was all merely the path we chose ourselves, that it was an exertion of strength, effort, and discipline which was unnecessary, even very dangerous? For, after all, everything was already prepared and fulfilled by grace! The glowing wick was mercilessly extinguished. It was unmerciful to speak to such people since they, confused by such a cheap offer, were forced to leave the path to which Christ called them clutching instead at cheap grace. Cheap grace would permanently prevent them from recognizing costly grace. It could not happen any other way but that possessing cheap grace would mislead weaklings to suddenly feel strong, yet in reality, they had lost their power for obedience and discipleship. The word of cheap grace has ruined more Christians than any commandment about works.

—from *Discipleship* 54–55

New Beatitudes

Our church's predicament is proving more and more clearly to be a question of how we are to live as Christians today. Blessed are they who already stand at the end of the path on which we wish to embark and perceive with amazement what really seems inconceivable: that grace is costly, precisely because it is pure grace, because it is God's grace in Jesus Christ. Blessed are they who by simply following Jesus Christ are overcome by this grace, so that with humble spirit they may praise the grace of Christ which alone is effective. Blessed are they who, in the knowledge of such grace, can live in the world without losing themselves in it. In following Christ their heavenly home has become so certain that they are truly free for life in this world. Blessed are they for whom following Jesus Christ means nothing other than living from grace and for whom grace means following Christ. Blessed are they who in this sense have become Christians, for whom the word of grace has been merciful.

—from *Discipleship* 55–56

Finding God in the Known

Weizsacker's book *The World View of Physics* is still keeping me very busy. It has again brought home to me quite clearly how wrong it is to use God as a stopgap for the incompleteness of our knowledge. If in fact the frontiers of knowledge are being pushed further and further back (and that's bound to be the case), then God is being pushed back with them, and is therefore continually in retreat. We are to find God in what we know, not in what we don't know; God wants us to realize the divine presence, not in unsolved problems but in those that are solved. That is true of the relationship between God and scientific knowledge, but it is also true of the wider human problems of death, suffering, and guilt.

—from *A Testament to Freedom* 506

God as the Stopgap

It is now possible to find, even for these questions [of death, suffering, and guilt], human answers that take no account whatever of God. In point of fact, people deal with these questions without God (it has always been so), and it is simply not true to say that only Christianity has the answers to them. As to the idea of "solving" problems, it may be that the Christian answers are just as unconvincing—or convincing—as any others. Here again, God is no stopgap; God must be recognized at the center of life, not when we are at the end of our resources; it is God's will to be recognized in life, and not only when death comes; in health and vigor, and not only in suffering; in our activities, and not only in sin. The ground for this lies in the revelation of God in Jesus Christ. He is the center of life, and he certainly didn't "come" to answer our unsolved problems. From the center of life certain questions, and their answers, are seen to be wholly irrelevant (I'm thinking of the judgment pronounced on Job's friends). In Christ there are no "Christian problems."

—from *A Testament to Freedom* 506

A Religion of Redemption

The decisive factor is said to be that in Christianity the hope of resurrection is proclaimed, and that that means the emergence of a genuine religion of redemption, the main emphasis now being on the far side of the boundary drawn by death. But it seems to me that this is just where the mistake and the danger lie. Redemption now means redemption from cares, distress, fears, and longings, from sin and death, in a better world beyond the grave. But is this really the essential character of the proclamation of Christ in the gospels and by Paul? I should say it is not. The difference between the Christian hope of resurrection and the mythological hope is that the former sends people back to their life on earth in a wholly new way which is even more sharply defined than it is in the Old Testament. Christians, unlike the devotees of the redemption myths, have no last line of escape available from earthly tasks and difficulties into the eternal, but, like Christ himself ("My God, why has thou forsaken me?"), they must drink the earthly cup to the dregs, and only in their doing so is the crucified and risen Lord with them, and they crucified and risen with Christ. This world must not be prematurely written off; in this the Old and New Testaments are at one. Redemption myths arise from human boundary experiences, but Christ takes hold of us at the center of our life.

—from *A Testament to Freedom* 507–508

Simplicity and Wisdom

Simplicity becomes wisdom. The person is wise who sees reality as it is, who sees into the depth of things. Only that person is wise who sees reality in God. Knowledge of reality is not just knowing external events, but seeing into the essence of things. The best-informed person is not the most intelligent. Precisely the best-informed people are in danger of missing the essential amid the variety. On the other hand, knowing an apparently trivial detail may often shed light on the depth of things. So the wise person will seek to obtain the best possible information about the course of events without becoming dependent on it. Wisdom is recognizing the significant within the factual. Wise people know the limited receptivity of reality for principles, because they know that reality is not built on principles, but rests on the living, creating God. So they also know that reality can be helped neither by the purest principles nor with the best will, but only by the living God. Principles are only tools in the hands of God; they will soon be thrown away when they are no longer useful. This liberated view of God and of reality, as it is real only in God, unites simplicity and wisdom. There is no true simplicity without wisdom, and no wisdom without simplicity.

—from *Ethics* 81–82

The Way of Duty

Men of *conscience* fend off all alone the superior power of predicaments that demand decision. But the dimensions of the conflicts in which they have to choose, counseled and supported by nothing but their own conscience, tear them to pieces. The countless respectable and seductive disguises and masks in which evil approaches them make their conscience anxious and unsure until they finally content themselves with an assuaged conscience instead of a good conscience, that is, until they deceive their own conscience in order not to despair. Those whose sole support is their conscience can never grasp that a bad conscience can be stronger and healthier than one that is deceived. The safe *way of duty* seems to offer escape from the bewildering profusion of possible decisions. What is commanded is grasped as the most certain. The person in command bears responsibility for the order, not the one who carries it out. However, those who limit themselves to duty will never venture a free action that rests solely on their own responsibility, the only sort of action that can meet evil at its heart and overcome it. People of duty must finally fulfill their duty even to the devil.

—from *Ethics* 79

On July 20, 1944, an assassination attempt is made on Hitler.

Private Virtue

Those, however, who take their stand in the world in their *very own freedom,* who value the necessary action more highly than their own untarnished conscience and reputation, who are prepared to sacrifice a barren principle to a fruitful compromise or a barren wisdom of the middle way to a fruitful radicalism, should take heed lest precisely their presumed freedom ultimately cause them to fall. They will easily consent to the bad, knowing full well that it is bad, in order to prevent the worse, and no longer be able to recognize that precisely the worse choice they wish to avoid may be the better one. Here lies the raw material of tragedy. In flight from public controversy this person or that reaches the sanctuary of a private virtuousness. Such people neither steal, nor murder, nor commit adultery, but do good according to their abilities. But in voluntarily renouncing public life, these people know exactly how to observe the permitted boundaries that shield them from conflict. They must close their eyes and ears to the injustice around them. Only at the cost of self-deception can they keep their private blamelessness clean from the stains of responsible action in the world. In all that they do, what they fail to do will not let them rest. Either they will be destroyed by this unrest, or they will become the most hypocritical of all Pharisees.

—from *Ethics* 79–80

Single-Minded Wisdom

Who may revile such failure and such collapse? Who of us does not know that we are also involved in one way or another? Reason, ethical fanaticism, conscience, duty, free responsibility, and quiet virtue are goods and convictions of a noble humanity. It is the best, with all they are and can do, who thus go under. . . . Only the person who combines simplicity with wisdom can endure. But what is simplicity? What is wisdom? How do the two become one? A person is simple who in the confusion, the distortion, and the inversion of all concepts keeps in sight only the single truth of God. This person has an undivided heart, and is not a double-psyche, a person of two souls (James 1:8). Because of knowing and having God, this person clings to the commandments, the judgment, and the mercy of God that proceed anew each day from the mouth of God. Not fettered by principles but bound by love for God, this person is liberated from the problems and conflicts of ethical decision, and is no longer beset by them. This person belongs to God and to God's will alone. The single-minded person does not also cast glances at the world while standing next to God and therefore is able, free, and unconstrained, to see the reality of the world.

—from *Ethics* 80–81

Who Am I?

Am I really what others say about me?
Or am I only what I know of myself?
Restless, yearning and sick, like a bird in its cage,
struggling for the breath of life,
as though someone were choking my throat;
hungering for colors, for flowers, for the songs of birds,
thirsting for kind words and human closeness,
shaking with anger at capricious tyranny and the pettiest slurs,
bedeviled by anxiety, awaiting great events that might never occur,
fearfully powerless and worried for friends far away,
weary and empty in prayer, in thinking, in doing,
weak, and ready to take leave of it all.

Who am I? This man or that other?
As I then this man today and tomorrow another?
Am I both all at once? An imposter to others,
but to me little more than a whining, despicable weakling?
Does what is in me compare to a vanquished army,
that flees in disorder before a battle already won?
Who am I? They mock me these lonely questions of mine.
Whoever I am, you know me, O God. You know I am yours.

—from *A Testament to Freedom* 514

Upsetting Love

The people who love, because they are freed through the truth of God, are the most revolutionary people on earth. They are the ones who upset all values; they are the explosives in human society. Such persons are the most dangerous. For they have recognized that people are untruthful in the extreme, and they are ready at any time, and just for the sake of love, to permit the light of truth to fall on them. This disturbance of peace, which comes to the world through these people, provokes the world's hatred. Therefore, the knight of truth and love is not the hero whom people worship and honor, who is free of enemies, but the one whom they cast out, whom they want to get rid of, whom they declare an outlaw, whom they kill. The way, which God's truth in the world has gone, leads to the cross.

—from *A Testament to Freedom* 206

Freedom and Truth

We know that all truth which exists in the presence of God must lead to the cross. The community that follows Christ must go with him to the cross. Because of their truth and freedom they will be hated by the world. Nor can a people find truth and freedom if they do not place themselves in the judgment of God's truth. Likewise, a people will remain in untruth and slavery until such time as they receive and continue to receive their truth and their freedom from God alone, until they know that truth and freedom lead to love; indeed, until they know that the way of love leads to the cross. If a people are really able to acknowledge this today, then they will be the only people who have the right to call themselves a free people, the only people that are not slaves to themselves, but who are the free servants of God's truth.

—from *A Testament to Freedom* 207

The Solution

What is behind the desire, which is awakening in Christendom throughout the world, to hear a message from the church to the world that offers solutions? It is essentially the following ideas: the social, economic, and political, etc., problems of the world are out of hand; the ideological and practical solutions being offered are all ineffectual; the world of technical progress has thus reached its limit; the car is stuck in the mud, the wheels are turning at top speed but cannot pull the car out; the problems are so universally human, both in their scope and their nature, that some quite fundamental remedy has become necessary; with respect to social, economic, political, sexual, and educational problems, the church has thus far failed; through its own fault it has given offense, which hinders people from believing its message. "Woe to those who give offense to one of these little ones . . ." (Matt. 18:6). A theologically correct Christian proclamation is not enough; neither are general ethical principles. What is necessary is a concrete directive in the concrete situation. The strength of the church's spirit is not yet exhausted. Christians throughout the world have grown closer to one another than ever before. Jointly they must tackle the task of proclaiming a message from the church. In short, the church is supposed to offer *solutions* for the world's unsolved problems, thus fulfilling its commission and restoring its authority.

—from *Ethics* 352–353

Solving the World's Problems

Is it really the task of the church today to offer the world solutions for its problems? Are there even Christian solutions to worldly problems? It apparently depends on what is meant by this. If one implies that Christianity has an answer to *all* social and political questions of the world, so that one would only have to listen to these answers to put the world in order, then this is obviously wrong. If one implies that from its vantage point Christianity has something specific to say about worldly things, then this is correct. . . . The kind of thinking that starts out with human problems, and then looks for solutions from that vantage point, has to be overcome—it is unbiblical. The way of Jesus Christ, and thus the way of all Christian thought, is not the way from the world to God but from God to the world. This means that the essence of the gospel does not consist in solving worldly problems, and also that this cannot be the essential task of the church. However, it does not follow from this that the church would have no task at all in this regard. But we will not recognize its legitimate task unless we first find the correct starting point.

—from *Ethics* 353–354, 356

The Message

The message of the church to the world can be none other than the word of God to the world. This word is: Jesus Christ, and salvation in this name. It is in Jesus Christ that God's relationship to the world is determined. We do not know any other relationship of God to the world apart from Jesus Christ. Therefore the church, too, has no relationship to the world other than through Jesus Christ. This means that the proper relationship of the church to the world does not derive from some natural law, or law of reason, or universal human rights, but *solely* from the gospel of Jesus Christ. The church's message to the world is the word about the coming of God in the flesh, about God's love for the world in the sending of God's Son, about God's judgment on unbelief. The church's message is the call to turn around, to believe in God's love in Christ, to prepare for the second coming of Christ, the coming kingdom of God. It is thus the word of redemption for all people. The message of God's love for the world places the church-community into a relationship of *responsibility* for the world. In both word and deed, the church-community has to witness to the world concerning its faith in Christ, to work on removing any offense, and to make room for the gospel in the world. Wherever this responsibility is denied, Christ is denied; for it is the responsibility that corresponds to God's love of the world.

—from *Ethics* 356–357

One Word

There are not two sets of values, one for the world and one for Christians. Rather, there is only the *one* word of God, demanding faith and obedience, which is valid for all people. It would also be wrong if the proclamation to the world placed greater emphasis on the "fighting for rights," while the proclamation to the church community placed more emphasis on giving up rights. *Both* are valid for the world and for the church-community. The assertion that it is not possible to govern with the Sermon on the Mount springs from a misunderstanding of the Sermon on the Mount. Fighting or retreating, a government may also honor God, and the proclamation of the church is concerned only with that. It is never the task of the church to preach to the state the message of the natural instinct for self-preservation, but only obedience toward what is owed to God. These are two different messages. The proclamation of the church to the world can always only be Jesus Christ in both law and gospel.

—from *Ethics* 359–360

Sunset Forgiveness

It is an old custom of the monasteries that by set practice in the daily evening worship the abbot asks his brothers to forgive him for all the sins of omission and wrongdoings committed against them. After the brothers assure him of their forgiveness, they like-wise ask the abbot to forgive them for their sins of omission and wrongdoings and receive his forgiveness. "Do not let the sun go down on your anger" (Eph. 4:26). It is a decisive rule of every Christian community that every division that the day has caused must be healed in the evening. It is perilous for the Christian to go to bed with an unreconciled heart. Therefore, it is a good idea especially to include the request for mutual forgiveness in every evening's prayers, so that reconciliation can be achieved and renewal of the community established.

—from *Life Together* 79

The End of the Day

In all the old evening prayers, it is striking how frequently we encounter their plea for preservation during the night from the devil, from terror and from an evil, sudden death. The ancients were keenly aware of human helplessness while sleeping, the kinship of sleep with death, and the devil's cunning in causing our downfall when we are defenseless. . . . Most remarkable and profound is the ancient church's request that, when our eyes are closed in sleep, God may nevertheless keep our hearts alert to God. It is a prayer that God may dwell with us and in us, even when we feel and know nothing, that God may keep our hearts pure and holy in spite of all the worries and temptations of the night, that God may prepare our hearts to hear the call at any time and, like the boy Samuel, answer even in the night, "Speak, Lord, for your servant is listening" (1 Sam. 3:10). Even while sleeping we are in the hands of God or in the power of the evil one. Even while we sleep, God can perform miracles upon us or the evil one can cause devastation in us. So we pray in the evening: "Though our eyes in sleep will close, / May our hearts in you repose, / Protect us, God, with your right arm, / And shield our souls from sin's cruel harm" (Luther). But the word of the Psalter stands over the morning and the evening: "Yours is the day, yours also the night" (Ps. 74:16).

—from *Life Together* 79–80

August

Hope for the Future

For most people, the compulsory abandonment of planning for the future means that they are forced back into living just for the moment, irresponsibly, frivolously, or resignedly; some few dream longingly of better times to come, and try to forget the present. We find both these courses equally impossible, and there remains for us only the very narrow way, often extremely difficult to find, of living every day as if it were our last, and yet living in faith and responsibility as though there were to be a great future: "Houses and fields and vineyards shall again be bought in this land" proclaims Jeremiah (32:15), in paradoxical contrast to his prophecies of woe, just before the destruction of the holy city. It is a sign from God and a pledge of a fresh start and a great future, just when all seems black. Thinking and acting for the sake of the coming generation, but being ready to go any day without fear or anxiety—that, in practice, is the spirit in which we are forced to live. It is not easy to be brave and keep that spirit alive, but it is imperative.

—from *Letters and Papers from Prison* 15

Good from Evil

I believe that God can and will bring good out of evil, even out of the greatest evil. For that purpose God needs men and women who make the best use of everything. I believe that God will give us all the strength we need to help us resist in all time of distress. But God never gives it in advance, lest we should rely on ourselves and not on God alone. A faith such as this should allay all our fears for the future. I believe that even our mistakes and shortcomings are turned to good account, and that it is no harder for God to deal with them than with our supposedly good deeds. I believe that God is no timeless fate, but that God waits for and answers sincere prayers and responsible actions.

—from *Letters and Papers from Prison* II

On August 2, 1934, Hitler is made chancellor and president of Germany.

Blind to Evil

That evil appears in the form of light, of beneficence, of faithfulness, of renewal, that it appears in the form of historical necessity, of social justice, is for the commonsense observer a clear confirmation of its profound evilness. Ethical theorists, on the other hand, are blinded by it. With their preconceived concepts they cannot grasp what is real, let alone seriously encounter something whose essence and power they don't even recognize. Those who are committed to an ethical agenda are compelled to a senseless waste of their energies. Even their martyrdom becomes neither a source of strength for their cause nor a threat to those who are evil. But, remarkably enough, not only the ethical theorists committed to an agenda miss their opponent, but those who are evil are hardly able to recognize their rivals. They fall into each other's traps. We experience and recognize ethical reality not by craftiness, not by knowing all the tricks, but only by standing straightforwardly in the truth of God and by looking to that truth with eyes that it makes simple and wise.

—from *Ethics* 77–78

Such a Time as This

We have grown up with the experience of our parents and grand-parents that people can and must plan, develop, and shape their own lives, and that life has a purpose, about which people must make up their minds, and which they must then pursue with all their strength. But we have learned by experience that we cannot plan even for the coming day, that what we have built up is being destroyed overnight, and that our life, in contrast to that of our parents, has become formless or even fragmentary. In spite of that, I can only say that I have no wish to live in any other time than our own, even though it is so inconsiderate of our outward well-being.

—from *Letters and Papers from Prison* 157

Growing Clarity

I have often wondered lately why we grow insensitive to hardships in the course of time. When I think how I felt for weeks a year ago, it strikes me very much. I now see the same things quite differently. To put it down to nature's self-protection does not seem to me adequate; I am more inclined to think that it may come from a clearer and more sober estimate of our own limitations and possibilities, which makes it possible for us genuinely to love our neighbor; as long as we let our imagination run riot, love of one's neighbor remains something vague and abstract. Today I can take a calmer view of other people, their predicaments and needs, and so I am better able to help them. I would speak of clarification rather than of insensitiveness; but of course, we are always having to try to change one into the other. I do not think we need reproach ourselves just because our feelings grow cooler and calmer in the course of time, though, of course, we must always be alive to the danger of not seeing the wood for the trees and keep a warm heart as well as a cool head.

—from *Letters and Papers from Prison* 137

Moral Memory

Something that repeatedly puzzles me as well as other people is how quickly we forget about our impressions of a night's bombing. Even a few minutes after the all clear, almost everything that we had just been thinking about seems to vanish into thin air. With Luther a flash of lightning was enough to change the course of his life for years to come. Where is this "memory" today? Is not the loss of this "moral memory" (a horrid expression) responsible for the ruin of all obligations, of love, marriage, friendship, and loyalty? Nothing sticks fast, nothing holds firm; everything is here today and gone tomorrow. But the good things of life—truth, justice, and beauty—all great accomplishments need time, constancy, and "memory," or they degenerate. Those who feel neither responsibility toward the past nor desire to shape the future are those who "forgets" and I do not know how one can really get at such people and bring them to their senses. Every word, even if it impresses them for the moment, goes in at one ear and out at the other. What is to be done about them?

—from *Letters and Papers from Prison* 109–110

Law and Grace

My thoughts and feelings seem to be getting more and more like those of the Old Testament, and in recent months I have been reading the Old Testament much more than the New. It is only when one knows the unutterability of the name of God that one can utter the name of Jesus Christ; it is only when one loves life and the earth so much that without them everything seems to be over that one can believe in the resurrection and a new world; it is only when one submits to God's law that one can speak of grace; and it is only when God's wrath and vengeance are hanging as grim realities over the heads of one's enemies that something of what it means to love and forgive them can touch our hearts.

—from *Letters and Papers from Prison* 86

Morning Prayers

O God, early in the morning I cry to thee.
Help me to pray
And to concentrate my thoughts on thee;
I cannot do this alone.

In me there is darkness,
But with thee there is light;
I am lonely, but thou leavest me not;
I am feeble in heart, but with thee there is help;
I am restless, but with thee there is peace.
In me there is bitterness, but with thee there is patience;
I do not understand thy ways,
But thou knowest the way for me.

O heavenly Father,
I praise and thank thee
For the peace of the night;
I praise and thank thee for this new day;
I praise and thank thee for all thy goodness
and faithfulness throughout my life.

—from *Letters and Papers from Prison* 72–73

Patience

The significance of patience in the New Testament is quite striking. Only the patient person received the promise (Matt. 24:13),
only the patient person brings forth good fruit (Luke 8:15). A faith
which does not become patience is inauthentic, unusable. Faith
must be proved. It can only be proved in suffering. Only suffering
and endurance will produce the "perfect work" (James 1:3ff). If
we remember that the word faith already contains the element of
faithfulness, we shall not be surprised at the close connection
between faith and patience. There is patience only "in Jesus"
(Rev. 1:9) for Jesus was patient as he bore the cross. Hebrews 12:2
describes Jesus's way of the cross as a way of endurance, of patience.
For us, endurance means to stand in the fellowship of Christ's suffering (1 Cor. 1:6ff), and thereby to gain assurance. If we share in
the patience of Jesus, we shall ourselves become patient and we
will finally have a share in his kingdom (2 Tim. 2:12). The way to
patience leads through discipline (2 Peter 1:6). The freer we are
from ease and indolence and personal claims, the more ready we
shall be for patience.

—from *A Testament to Freedom* 443–444

The God of Patience

We can remain united only if we remain patient. Impatience makes for division. And unfortunately it cannot be denied that all those who have already gone their own way through impatience have made the struggle and test of patience still more difficult for the other brethren. Impatience disrupts community. In the view of the gospel, it is not just a minor, venial, bad habit; it is a failure in the testing of faith. "Now the God of patience"—the God who endured in Jesus Christ and helps us to endure—gives you "one mind"—to stand by one another in these hours of testing, to come closer to one another, to strengthen and help one another. It is grim if anyone departs at such a time. But our patience depends not upon people, but upon Jesus Christ and his patience on the cross. He bore the impatience of all people and so can forgive them. "One mind," i.e., not this way today and another tomorrow: remain firm by what you already know, remain constant, show yourselves faithful. How little importance we attach to constancy, firmness, and faithfulness! In the Scriptures they are right at the top of the list.

—from *A Testament to Freedom* 444

As Though There Were No God

We cannot be honest unless we recognize that we have to live in the world *etsi deus non daretur*. And this is just what we do recognize—before God! God himself compels us to recognize it. So our coming of age leads us to a true recognition of our situation before God. God would have us know that we must live as people who manage our lives without God. The God who is with us is the God who forsakes us (Mark 15:34). The God who lets us live in the world without the working hypothesis of God is the God before whom we stand continually. Before God and with God we live without God. God lets the divine self be pushed out of the world onto the cross. God is weak and powerless in the world, and that is precisely the way, the only way, in which God is with us and helps us. Matthew 8:17 makes it quite clear that Christ helps us, not by virtue of his omnipotence, but by virtue of his weakness and suffering.

—from *A Testament to Freedom* 508

The Suffering God

Jesus asked in Gethsemane, "Could you not watch with me one hour?" That is a reversal of what the religious person expects from God. We are summoned to share in God's sufferings at the hands of a godless world. We must therefore really live in the godless world, without attempting to gloss over or explain its ungodliness in some religious way or other. We must live a "secular" life, and thereby share in God's sufferings. We *may* live a "secular" life (as one who has been freed from false religious obligations and inhibitions). To be a Christian does not mean to be religious in a particular way, to make something of oneself (a sinner, a penitent, or a saint) on the basis of some method or other, but to be a person— not a type of person, but the person that Christ creates in us. It is not the religious act that makes the Christian, but participation in the sufferings of God in the secular life. That is *metanoia*: not in the first place thinking about one's own needs, problems, sins, and fears, but allowing oneself to be caught up into the way of Jesus Christ, into the messianic event.

—from *A Testament to Freedom* 508–509

Irreligion

My recent activity, which has been predominantly in the secular sphere, keeps making me think. I'm amazed that I live, and can live, all day long without the Bible. If I were to force myself to it, I would regard my action, not as obedience, but as autosuggestion. I understand that such autosuggestion could be, and is, a great help, but I would be afraid in this way of falsifying a real experience and ultimately not finding any authentic help. When I open the Bible again, it is new, and more cheering than ever, and I would love to preach just once more. I know that I need only open my own books to hear what can be said against all this. I don't want to justify myself, but I recognize that "spiritually" I have had much richer times. I detect that a rebellion against all things "religious" is growing in me. Often it amounts to an instinctive horror—which is certainly not good. I'm not religious by nature. But I have to think continually of God and Christ; authenticity, life, freedom, and mercy mean a great deal to me. It is just their religious manifestations which are so unattractive. Do you understand? These are no new ideas and insights, but since I feel a knot is about to explode within me here, I'm letting these things have their head and not resisting them.

—from *A Testament to Freedom* 499

Our Daily Bread

Christian community at the table also signifies obligation. It is our daily bread that we eat, not my own. We share our bread. Thus we are firmly bound to one another not only in the Spirit, but with our whole physical being. The one bread that is given to our community unites us in a firm covenant. Now no one must hunger as long as the other has bread, and whoever shatters this community of our bodily life also shatters the community of the Spirit. Both are inextricably linked together. . . . The breaking of bread together teaches Christians that here they still eat the perishable bread of the earthly pilgrimage. But if they share this bread with one another, they will also one day receive together imperishable bread in the Father's house. "Blessed is the one who will eat bread in the reign of God" (Luke 14:15).

—from *Life Together* 73–74

The Free Work of God

Then God said, "Let us make humankind in our image, according to our likeness." Human beings are to proceed from God as the ultimate, the new, and as the image of God in God's works. There is no transition here from somewhere or other; here there is new creation. This has nothing at all to do with Darwinism. Quite independently of this, the human person remains the new, free, and unconstricted work of God. We certainly have no wish to deny our connection with the animal world: rather it is just the opposite. But we are very anxious not to lose the unique relationship of humans and God in the process. In our concern with the origin and nature of human beings, it would be a hopeless effort for us to attempt to make a gigantic leap back into the world of the lost beginning. It is hopeless for us to want to know for ourselves what the original human being was like, to identify one's own ideal of the human with the creational reality of God. Such attempts fail to understand that we can know about the original human beings only if we start from Christ. This hopeless, though understandable, attempt has again and again delivered the church up to unbridled speculation on this dangerous point. Only in the middle, as those who live from Christ, do we know the beginning.

—from *A Testament to Freedom* 106

A Free Creation

God creates God's image on earth in the human. This means that humans are like the Creator in that they are free. Actually one is free only through God's creation, by means of the Word of God; one is free for the worship of the Creator. In the language of the Bible, freedom is not something persons have for themselves but something they have for others. No one enjoys freedom "in itself," that is, in a vacuum, the same way that one may be musical, intelligent, or blind as such. Freedom is not a quality of the human person. Nor is it an ability, a disposition, a kind of being that somehow deeply germinates in a person. Whoever scrutinizes the human to discover freedom will find nothing of it. Why? Because freedom is not a quality that can be discovered. It is not a possession, a presence, or an object. Nor is it a pattern for existence. Rather, it is a relationship; otherwise, it is nothing. Indeed, it is a relationship between two persons. Being free means "being free for the other," because the other has bound me to himself or herself. Only in relationship with the other am I free.

—from *A Testament to Freedom* 106–107

Real Freedom

No substantial or individualistic concept of freedom has the ability to encompass freedom. Freedom is something over which I have no control as a possession. It is simply the event, the experience, that happens to me through the other. If we ask how we know this, or whether this is not just another speculation about the beginning that results from being in the middle, we can answer that it is the message of the gospel itself, that God's freedom has bound us to the divine self, that God's free grace becomes real only in this relationship with us, and that God does not will to be free for the divine self but for man and woman. Because God in Christ is free for us humans, because God does not hoard freedom for the divine self we can envision freedom only as a "being free for." For us who live in the middle through Christ and know our humanity in his resurrection, that God is free means nothing more than that we are free for God.

—from *A Testament to Freedom* 107

Jesus the Word

Only if I know who does the work can I have access to the work of Christ. Here everything depends upon knowing the person in order to recognize the work. If he was an idealistic founder of a religion, I can be elevated by his work and stimulated to follow his example. But my sin is not forgiven, God remains angry, and I am still in the power of death. Then the work of Jesus drives me to despair about myself, because I cannot follow his example. But if Jesus is the Christ, the Word of God, then I am not primarily called to do the things that he does; I am met in his work as one who cannot possibly do the work he does. It is through his work that I recognize the gracious God. My sin is forgiven, I am no longer in death, but in life. All this depends upon the person of Christ, whether his work perishes in the world of death or abides in a new world of life.

—from *A Testament to Freedom* 114

Christ the Center

That Christ is the center of our existence does not mean that he is central in our personality, our thinking, and our feeling. Christ is also our center when he stands, in terms of our consciousness, on our periphery, also when Christian piety is displaced to the periphery of our being. The statement made about his centrality is not psychological, but has the character of an ontological and theological statement. It does not refer to our personality, but to our being a person before God. The center of the person cannot be demonstrated. The truth of the statement that Christ is our center does not allow for confirmation by proof. For it concerns the center in which we believe within the space of the person in whom we believe. In the fallen world the center is also the boundary. Humans stand between law and fulfillment. They have the law, but cannot fulfill it. Now Christ stands where humans have failed before the law. Christ as the center means that he is the fulfillment of the law. So he is in turn the boundary and the judgment of the human, but also the beginning of our new existence, its center. Christ as the center of human existence means that he is our judgment and justification.

—from *A Testament to Freedom* 117

The Present Age

The intention should not be to justify Christianity in this present age, but *to justify the present age before the Christian message.* Interpretation then means that the present age is brought before the forum of the Christian message, in other words that the question is of the fact, the value (!) of the Christian message instead of being of the character of the present age, as in the false concept of relevance. True relevance lies in this question of the fact. It is felt of the *fact itself* that where it is really expressed it is in itself completely and utterly relevant; it therefore needs no other special act of interpretation, because the interpretation is achieved in the fact itself. This, however, is only so because *this* fact is the concern of the New Testament, because the fact here is Christ, and his word. Where Christ is spoken of in the word of the New Testament, relevance is achieved. *The relevant* is not where the present age announces its claim before Christ, but where the present age stands before the claims of Christ, for the concept of the present age is determined not by a temporal definition but by the Word of Christ as the Word of God.

—from *A Testament to Freedom* 151–152

The Concerns of the Church

Because the church is concerned with God, the Holy Spirit, and God's Word, it is therefore not specially concerned with religion, but with *obedience* to the Word, with the *work* of the Father, i.e., with the completion of the new creation in the Spirit. It is not the religious question or religious concern of any form which constitute the church—from a human point of view—but obedience to the Word of the new creation of grace. In other words, the church is constituted not by religious formulae, by dogma, but by the practical doing of what is commanded. The pure reaching of the gospel is not a religious concern, but a desire to execute the will of God for a new creation. In the church, the Holy Spirit and obedience take the place of "the religious."

—from *A Testament to Freedom* 155

In Step with God

I believe that we ought so to love and trust God in our lives, and in all the good things that God sends us, that when the time comes (but not before!) we may go to God with love, trust, and joy. But, to put it plainly, for a man in his wife's arms to be hankering after the other world is, in mild terms, a piece of bad taste, and not God's will. We ought to find and love God in what we are actually given; if it pleases God to allow us to enjoy some overwhelming earthly happiness, we must not try to be more pious than God and allow our happiness to be corrupted by presumption and arrogance, and by unbridled religious fantasy which is never satisfied with what God gives. God will see to it that those who find the Divine in earthly happiness and thank God for it do not lack reminder that earthly things are transient, that it is good for them to attune their hearts to what is eternal, and that sooner or later there will be times when they can say in all sincerity, "I wish I were home." But everything has its time, and the main thing is that we keep step with God, and do not keep pressing on a few steps ahead—nor keep dawdling a step behind.

—from *Letters and Papers from Prison* 94

The Friend

When the spirit touches
mans heart and brow
with thoughts that are lofty, bold, serene,
so that with clear eyes he will face the world
as a free man may;
when then the spirit gives birth to action
by which alone we stand or fall;
when from the sane and resolute action
rises the work that gives a man's life
content and meaning—
then would that man,
lonely and actively working,
know of the spirit that grasps and befriends him,
like waters clear and refreshing
where the spirit is cleansed from the dust
and cooled from the heat that oppressed him,
steeling himself in the hour of fatigue—
like a fortress to which, from confusion and danger,
the spirit returns,
wherein he finds refuge and comfort and strengthening,
is a friend to a friend.

—from *Letters and Papers from Prison* 210

On August 23, 1944, Bonhoeffer writes his last letter to his best friend,
Eberhard Bethge.

Confronting Sin

When Christians live together, at some time and in some way it must come to the point that one Christian personally declares God's Word and will to another. It is inconceivable that the things that are most important to each individual should not be discussed with one another. It is un-Christian when one person knowingly denies another this decisive service. If we cannot bring ourselves to say the necessary word, we will have to ask ourselves whether we are not still seeing other Christians clothed in a human dignity that we think we dare not touch, and thus whether we are not forgetting the most important thing—that they, too, no matter how old or high ranking or distinguished they may be, are still persons like us, sinners crying out for God's grace. They have the same great troubles that we have, and need help, comfort, and for-giveness as we do. The basis on which Christians can speak to one another is that each knows the other as a sinner who, even given all one's human renown, is forlorn and lost if not given help. This does not mean that the others are being disparaged or dishonored. Rather, we are paying them the only real honor a human being has, namely, that as sinners they share in God's grace and glory, that they are children of God.

—from *Life Together* 104

Growing Together

We talk to one another about the help we both need. We admonish one another to go the way Christ bids us to go. We warn one another against the disobedience that is our undoing. We are gentle and we are firm with one another, for we know both God's kindness and God's firmness. Why should we be afraid of one another since both of us have only God to fear? Why should we think that another Christian would not understand us when we understand very well what was meant when somebody spoke God's comfort or God's admonition to us, even in words that were inept and awkward? Or do we really believe there is a single person in this world who does not need either comfort or admonition? If so, then why has God given us the gift of Christian community?

—from *Life Together* 104–105

Speaking the Truth

The more we learn to allow the other to speak the Word to us, to accept humbly and gratefully even severe reproaches and admonitions, the more free and to the point we ourselves will be in speaking. One who because of sensitivity and vanity rejects the serious words of another Christian cannot speak the truth in humility to others. Such a person is afraid of being rejected and feeling hurt by another's words. Sensitive, irritable people will always become flatterers, and very soon they will come to despise and slander other Christians in their community. But humble people will cling to both truth and love. They will stick to the Word of God and let it lead them to others in their community. They can help others through the Word because they seek nothing for themselves and have no fears for themselves.

—from *Life Together* 105

Loving Admonition

When another Christian falls into obvious sin, an admonition is imperative, because God's Word demands it. The practice of discipline in the community of faith begins with friends who are close to one another. Words of admonition and reproach must be risked when a lapse from God's Word in doctrine or life endangers a community that lives together, and with it the whole community of faith. Nothing can be more cruel than that leniency which abandons others to their sin. Nothing can be more compassionate than that severe reprimand which calls another Christian in one's community back from the path of sin. When we allow nothing but God's Word to stand between us, judging and helping, it is a service of mercy, an ultimate offer of genuine community. Then it is not we who are judging; God alone judges, and God's judgment is helpful and healing. After all, we can only serve other Christians; we can never place ourselves above them. We serve them even when we must speak the judging and sundering Word of God to them, even when in obedience to God we must break off community with them. We know that it is not our human love that enables us to remain devoted to others, but God's love that comes to them only through judgment.

—from *Life Together* 105–106

Belonging to Christ

"Whoever is not against us is for us" (Mark 9:40). Christ draws the boundaries of who and what belongs to him more generously than his disciples wish to do and actually do themselves. In the concrete case to which the saying of Jesus refers, someone drives out demons in the name of Jesus without personally being a disciple and follower of Jesus. Jesus prohibits his disciples from stopping him; for "no one who does a miracle in my name will tend to slander me soon afterward" (verse 39). Wherever the name of Jesus is still mentioned—even if in ignorance, even if only in recognizing its objective power without following it with personal obedience, even if with stammering and embarrassment—there this name creates a space for itself to which the slandering of Jesus has no access; there the power of Christ still has a sphere of influence; there one ought not interfere, but allow the name of Jesus Christ to do its work. . . . Wherever the name of Jesus Christ is pronounced, it is both protection and claim. This is true for all those who in their struggle for justice, truth, humanity, and freedom have once again learned to utter the name of Jesus Christ, even if only with hesitation and genuine timidity. This name provides safety for them and the noble values they defend. At the same time, this name claims both them and these values.

—from *Ethics* 342

Boundaryless Boundaries

"Whoever is not for me is against me" (Matt. 12:30). It is the same Jesus who speaks this word; and while abstract reasoning finds an irreconcilable contradiction here, both sayings of Jesus belong, in reality, necessarily together. Once again we have the living experience on our side: we are talking about the time when, under the pressure of anti-Christian powers, small confessing congregations gathered and had to seek a clear decision for or against Christ through strict discipline of doctrine and life. In their struggle these confessing congregations were forced to recognize that the very neutrality of many Christians was the gravest danger that would lead to the disintegration and dissolution of the church, indeed, that it was essentially hostility toward Christ. When the exclusive demand for an unequivocal confession of Christ caused the band of confessing Christians to become smaller and smaller, then the saying, "Whoever is not for me is against me," became a concrete experience for the Christian community. Thus it gained, precisely through this concentration on what is essential, an inner freedom and openness that protected it from all anxious efforts to erect boundaries. So it gathered people who had traveled from afar, and to them it could not deny its community and protection. Wounded justice, oppressed truth, humiliated humanity, violated freedom—all these now sought the Christian community, or rather its Lord, Jesus Christ. And thus it came to know the other saying of Jesus as a living experience: "Whoever is not against us is with us."

—from *Ethics* 343–344

Christ in Culture

It is not Christ who has to justify himself before the world by acknowledging the values of justice, truth, and freedom. Instead, it is these values that find themselves in need of justification, and their justification is Jesus Christ alone. It is not a "Christian culture" that still has to make the name of Jesus Christ acceptable to the world; instead, the crucified Christ has become the refuge, justification, protection, and claim for these higher values and their defenders who have been made to suffer. It is with the Christ, persecuted and suffering together with his church-community, that justice, truth, humanity, and freedom seek refuge. It is the Christ who is unable to find shelter in the world, the Christ of the manger and the cross who is cast out of the world, who is the shelter to whom one flees for protection; only thus is the full breadth of Christ's power revealed. The cross of Christ makes both sayings true: "Whoever is not for me is against me" and "Whoever is not against us is for us."

—from *Ethics* 345–346

Contempt for Humanity

There is a very real danger of our drifting into an attitude of contempt for humanity. We know quite well that we have no right to do so, and that it would lead us into the most sterile relation to our fellow human beings. The following thoughts may keep us from such a temptation. It means that we at once fall into the worst blunders of our opponents. The person who despises another will never be able to make anything of that person. Nothing that we despise in the other person is entirely absent from ourselves. We often expect from others more than we are willing to do ourselves. Why have we hitherto thought so intemperately about human frailty and temptability? We must learn to regard people less in the light of what they do or omit to do, and more in the light of what they suffer. The only profitable relationship to others—and especially to our weaker brothers and sisters—is one of love, and that means the will to be in community with them. God did not despise humanity, but became a human for humanity's sake.

—from *Letters and Papers from Prison* 9

September

Grace Alone

The origin and essence of all Christian life are consummated in the one event that the Reformation has called the justification of the sinner by grace alone. It is not what a person is per se, but what a person is in this event, that gives us insight into the Christian life. Here the length and breadth of human life are concentrated in one moment, one point; the whole of life is embraced in this event. What happens here? Something ultimate that cannot be grasped by anything we are, or do, or suffer. The dark tunnel of human life, which was barred within and without and was disappearing ever more deeply into an abyss from which there is no exit, is powerfully torn open; the word of God bursts in. In this saving light, people recognize God and their neighbors for the first time. The labyrinth of their previous lives collapses. They become free for God and for one another. They realize that there is a God who loves and accepts them, that alongside them stand others whom God loves equally, and that there is a future with the triune God and God's church-community. Each believes, loves, hopes. The past and future of the whole of life flow together in God's presence.

—from *Ethics* 146–147

No Longer Lost

The whole of the past is embraced by the word "forgiveness"; the whole of the future is preserved in the faithfulness of God. Past sin has been sunk in the depths of God's love in Jesus Christ and overcome; the future will be, without sin, a life born of God (1 John 3:9). This life knows itself stretched and sustained from one eternal foundation to another, from its election before the time of the world toward eternal salvation to come. This life knows itself as a member of a church and of a creation that sings the praises of the triune God. All this happens when Christ comes to each person. In Christ all this is truth and reality. Precisely because it is not a dream, the life of a person who has encountered Christ's presence is no longer lost, but has become justified, by grace alone.

—from *Ethics* 147

Faith Alone

[We are justified] not only by grace alone, but also by faith alone. So Scripture and the Reformation teach. Not love or hope, but only faith justifies a life. It is faith alone that sets life on a new foundation, and only on this new foundation can I live justified before God. This foundation is the living, dying, and rising of the Lord Jesus Christ. Without this foundation a life before God is unjustified; it is surrendered to death and damnation. The justification of my life before God is to live because of and toward the living, dying, and rising of Jesus Christ. Faith means to find, hold to, and cast my anchor on this foundation and so to be held by it. Faith means to base life on a foundation outside myself, on an eternal and holy foundation, on Christ. Faith means to be captivated by the gaze of Jesus Christ; one sees nothing but him. Faith means to be torn out of imprisonment in one's own ego, liberated by Jesus Christ. Faith is letting something happen, and only therein is it an activity. Yet both words together cannot adequately express its mystery. Faith alone is certainty; everything outside of faith is subject to doubt. Jesus Christ alone is the certainty of faith. I believe the Lord Jesus Christ who tells me that my life is justified. So there is no way toward the justification of my life other than faith alone.

—from *Ethics* 147–148

The Company of Faith

Faith is never alone. As surely as it is the genuine presence of Christ, so surely love and hope are with it. Faith would be a false, illusory, hypocritical self-invention which never justifies, were it not accompanied by love and hope. It would be a rote-learned repetition of articles of faith, a dead faith, if the works of repentance and love did not accompany it. Faith and evil intentions cannot exist together even for an instant. Everything is given to me in the event of justification, but only faith justifies. All that Christ is and has is made mine in the encounter with Christ, but my life is justified only by that which belongs to Christ and never by what became mine. So heaven is torn open above us humans, and the joyful message of God's salvation in Jesus Christ rings out from heaven to earth as a cry of joy. I believe, and in believing I receive Christ, I have everything. I live before God.

—from *Ethics* 148

Christ in Between

It is true, there is something which comes between persons called by Christ and the given circumstances of their natural lives. But it is not someone unhappily contemptuous of life; it is not some law of piety. Instead, it is life and the gospel itself; it is Christ himself. In becoming human, he put himself between me and the given circumstances of the world. I cannot go back. He is in the middle. He has deprived those whom he has called of every immediate connection to those given realities. He wants to be the medium; everything should happen only through him. He stands not only between me and God, he also stands between me and the world, between me and other people and things.

—from *Discipleship* 93–94

Christ the Mediator

[Christ] is the mediator, not only between God and human persons, but also between person and person, and between person and reality. Because the whole world was created by him and for him (John 1:3; 1 Cor. 8:6; Heb. 1:2), he is the sole mediator in the world. Since Christ there has been no more unmediated relationship for the human person, neither to God nor to the world. Christ intends to be the mediator. To be sure, there are plenty of other gods which offer immediate access and, in fact, the world tries by all means to relate to persons immediately. But herein lies precisely its hostility to Christ, the mediator. Other gods and the world want to tear away from Christ what he deprived them of, namely, the ability to relate immediately to human persons.

—from *Discipleship* 94

The Call to Discipleship

To his first disciples Jesus was bodily present, speaking his word directly to them. But this Jesus died and is risen. How, then, does his call to discipleship reach us today? Jesus no longer walks past me in bodily form and calls, "Follow me," as he did to Levi, the tax collector. Even if I would be truly willing to listen, to leave everything behind, and to follow, what justification do I have for doing so? What for the first disciples was so entirely unambiguous is for me a decision that is highly problematic and fraught with uncertainty. . . . There is something wrong with . . . these questions. Every time we ask them, we place ourselves outside the living presence of the Christ. All of these questions refuse to take seriously that Jesus Christ is not dead but alive and still speaking to us today through the testimony of Scripture. He is present with us today, in bodily form and with his word. If we want to hear his call to discipleship, we need to hear it where Christ himself is present. It is within the church that Jesus Christ calls through his word and sacrament.

—from *Discipleship* 201–202

Morning Blessing

"Let the Word of Christ dwell in you richly" (Col. 3:16). The Old Testament day begins on one evening and ends with the sundown of the next evening. That is the time of expectation. The day of the New Testament church begins at sunrise in the early morning and ends with the dawning light of the next morning. That is the time of fulfillment, the resurrection of the Lord. At night Christ was born, a light in the darkness; noonday turned to night when Christ suffered and died on the cross. But early on Easter morning Christ emerged victorious from the grave. "Ere yet the dawn has filled the skies / Behold my Savior Christ arise, / He chases from us sin and night, / And brings us joy and life and light. Halleluia." So sang the church of the Reformation. Christ is the "Sun of righteousness," who has risen upon the expectant congregation (Mal. 4:2), and they who love him will be like the sun when it rises in its strength (Judges 5:31). The early morning belongs to the church of the risen Christ. At the break of light it remembers the morning on which death, the devil, and sin were brought low in defeat, and new life and salvation were given to human beings.

—from *Life Together* 48–49

God of Love

If you ask me: What is Christendom?—I answer: Christendom is the great congregation of people who humble themselves before God and who put all their hope and faith in the love and the help of God. Christendom is the community in which people stand for each other, as a brother stands for his brother. Christendom is one great people composed of persons of every country in concord in their faith and their love because there is One God, One Lord, One Spirit, One Hope. That is the marvelous mystery of the people of God. Above all differences of race, nationality, and custom there is an invisible community of the children of God. There each one prays for the others, be he or she American or German or African; here each one loves the others without reservation. Let us in this hour gratefully consider that we all belong to this church, that God has called us to be his children and made us brethren, that there cannot be any hate or enmity, but only the best will to understand each other. Otherwise we would not be worthy to bear the name of Christ, we would offend the glory of God, who is a God of love and not hate.

—from *A Testament to Freedom* 188

Assured Peace

For Christ it is not a question of changing the conditions of this world for the sake of our security and quiet. Still less ought we to think we are able to do away with the horror of war through political agreements that serve only to give expression to our sins. So long as the world is without God, there will be wars. For Christ, rather, it is a matter of our loving God and standing in discipleship to Jesus in whom we are called with the promise of blessedness to become witnesses for peace. This *discipleship of Christ* comes from and depends entirely on simple *faith*. On the other hand this faith is genuine only in discipleship. Thus believers are addressed and the world is judged by Christ's witness for peace. This faith must, however, be simple. Otherwise it produces mere reflection on itself, not obedience. The believer might also learn only the wrong slant on things; doing what is "correct" but not really engaged in discipleship that knows nothing of the fine distinction between good and evil. . . . There are, therefore, no human possibilities of assuring or organizing peace. Indeed, this human effort, using political means to achieve peace, can lead directly to the sins of domineering over an independent people. There is no assured peace. The Christian can aspire to peace only from faith. There is no direct achievement of brotherhood and sisterhood among people. There is access to one's enemies only through prayer to the Lord of all peoples and nations.

—from *A Testament to Freedom* 94

The Command of Love

We Christians are above all addressed by the command of love to the point that we ourselves must live in peace with every person, just like Christ when he preached peace to the community, exemplified in peace with one's brother and sister, with one's neighbor, with the Samaritan. Unless we have this peace, we cannot preach peace to people. Most who are annoyed at the world of peace among peoples, moreover, are already calling in question the love of enemies over against the personal enemy. When we wish to speak about the conditions for peace, therefore, we would do well always to keep before our eyes the fact that relationships between two nations bear close analogy to relationships between two individuals. The conditions that are opposed to peace are in the one as in the other relationship: lust for power, pride, inordinate desire for glory and honor, arrogance, feelings of inferiority, and strife over more living space and over one's "bread" or life. What is sin for an individual is never virtue for an entire people or nation. What is proclaimed as the gospel to the church, the congregation, and, thereby, the individual Christian, is spoken to the world as a judgment. When a people refuses to hear this command, then Christians are called forth from that people to give witness to peace. Let us take care, however, that we miserable sinners proclaim peace from a spirit of love and not from any zeal for security or from any mere political aim.

—from *A Testament to Freedom* 95

From Betrayal to Trust

There is hardly one of us who has not known what it is to be betrayed. The figure of Judas, which we used to find so difficult to understand, is now fairly familiar to us. The air that we breathe is so polluted by mistrust that it almost chokes us. But where we have broken through the layer of mistrust, we have been able to discover a confidence hitherto undreamed of. Where we trust, we have learned to put our very lives into the hands of others; in the face of all the different interpretations that have been put on our lives and actions, we have learned to trust unreservedly. We now know that only such confidence, which is always a venture, though a glad and positive venture, enables us really to live and work. We know that it is most reprehensible to sow and encourage mistrust, and that our duty is rather to foster and strengthen confidence wherever we can. Trust will always be one of the greatest, rarest, and happiest blessings of our life in a community, though it can emerge only on the dark background of a necessary mistrust. We have learned never to trust a scoundrel an inch, but to give ourselves to the trustworthy without reserve.

—from *Letters and Papers from Prison* 11–12

Adulthood

But is it not characteristic of adults, in contrast to an immature person, that their center of gravity is always where they actually are, and that the longing for the fulfillment of their wishes cannot prevent them from being their whole self, wherever they happen to be? The adolescent is never wholly in one place; that is one of the essential characteristics [of youth], else he would presumably be a dullard. There is a wholeness about the fully grown adult which enables a person to face an existing situation squarely. Adults may have their longings, but they keep them out of sight, and somehow master them; and the more they have to overcome in order to live fully in the present, the more they will have the respect and confidence of other people, especially the younger ones, who are still on the road that the adult has already traveled. Desires to which we cling closely can easily prevent us from being what we ought to be and can be; and on the other hand, desires repeatedly mastered for the sake of present duty make us richer. Lack of desire is poverty. Almost all the people whom I find in my present surroundings cling to their own desires, and so have no interest in others; they no longer listen, and they are incapable of loving their neighbor. I think that even in this place we ought to live as if we had no wishes and no future, and just be our true selves.

—from *Letters and Papers from Prison* 127

Gaining Composure

I see that composure is not part of my nature, but that I have to acquire it at the cost of repeated effort. In fact, natural composure is probably in most cases nothing but a euphemism for indifference and indolence, and to that extent it is not very estimable. I read in Lessing recently: "I am too proud to consider myself unlucky. Just clench your teeth and let your skiff sail where the wind and waves take it. Enough that I do not intend to upset it myself." Is this pride and teeth-clenching to be forbidden to the Christian, and replaced, shall we say, by a soft composure that gives way prematurely? Is there not also a kind of composure which proudly clenches its teeth, but is quite different from a dull, stolid, rigid, lifeless, mechanical submitting-to-something-I-can't-help? I think we honor God more if we gratefully accept the life that God gives us with all it's blessings, loving it and drinking it to the full, and also grieving deeply and sincerely when we have impaired or wasted any of the good things of life (some people denounce such an attitude, and think it is bourgeois, weak, and sensitive), than if we are insensitive to life's blessings and may therefore also be insensitive to pain.

—from *Letters and Papers from Prison* 103

A Historical Heritage

The concept of a historical heritage, bound to an awareness of temporality and resistant to all mythologizing, is only possible where thought, consciously or unconsciously, is determined by the entry of God into history at a definite place and time, in which God became human in Jesus Christ. Here history becomes serious, without being sanctified. God's Yes and God's No to history, as we understand it in the incarnation and crucifixion of Jesus Christ, bring a lasting and irremovable tension into every historical moment. Through the life and death of Jesus Christ, history becomes not the transient bearer of eternal values but, for the first time, thoroughly temporal. Precisely in its temporality, it is history affirmed by God. The inquiry about historical heritage is not, therefore, the timeless question of the eternally valid values of the past. Rather, it is here that human beings, placed in history, must give an accounting to themselves about the present time as it has been taken on by God in Christ.

—from *Ethics* 103–104

The Book of God

One simply cannot read the Bible like other books. We must be prepared really to question it. Only in this way is it revealed to us. Only if we await the final answer from it does it give that Word to us. The reason for this is that in the Bible God speaks to us. And we cannot simply reflect upon God from ourselves; rather, we must ask God. Only when we seek God does God answer. Naturally one can also read the Bible like any other book, as for example from the viewpoint of textual criticism, etc. There is certainly nothing to be said against this. Only that it is not the way that reveals the essence of the Bible, only its superficial surface. Just as we do not grasp the word of a person whom we love, in order to dissect it, but just as such a word is simply accepted and it then lingers with us all day long, simply as the word of this person whom we love, and just as the one who reveals himself to us as the one who has spoken to us in this word that move us ever more deeply in our hearts like Mary, so should we treat the Word of God. Only if we dare for once to enter into relationship with the Bible as the place where the God who loves us really speaks to us and will not leave us alone with our questions will we be happy with the Bible.

—from *A Testament to Freedom* 425

Finding God

If I am one who says where God shall be, so I will always find a God there who corresponds in some way to me, is pleasing to me, who belongs to my nature. If it is, however, God who speaks where God chooses to be, then that will probably be a place which does not at all correspond to my nature, which is not at all pleasing to me. But this place is the cross of Christ. And the one who will find him there must be with him under this cross, just as the Sermon on the Mount demands. This doesn't suit our nature at all but is completely counter to it. This, however, is the message of the Bible, not only in the New but also in the Old Testament (Is. 53!). In any event, Jesus and Paul intended this: with the cross of Jesus is the Scripture, that is, the Old Testament, fulfilled. The whole Bible will, therefore, be the Word in which God will allow the divine self to be discovered by us. This is no place which is pleasing or *a priori* sensible to us, but a place strange to us in every way and which is entirely contrary to us. But this is the very place God has chosen to encounter us.

—from *A Testament to Freedom* 425–426

Listening to God

So now I read the Bible in this way. I ask in every place: What is God saying to us here? I ask God to show us what God wants to say. Thus we are not at all permitted to seek after general, eternal truths which would correspond to our own "everlasting" nature and as such would be made evident. Rather, we seek the will of God who is entirely strange and contrary to us, whose ways are not our ways and whose thoughts are not our thoughts, who hides under the sign of the cross at which all our ways and thoughts come to an end. God is wholly other than the so-called eternal truth. That is always still our own thoughts of self and our wished-for life everlasting. God's Word, however, begins where God points us to the cross of Jesus at which all our ways and thoughts, also the so-called everlasting, converge, namely in death and God's judgment. . . . Since I have learned to read the Bible in this way—and that is not so very long ago—it becomes more wonderful to me every day. I read it every morning and evening, often also during the day. And every day I take for myself a text that I will have for the entire week and attempt to immerse myself entirely in it, in order to be able to really listen to it. I know that without this I would no longer be able to live properly. Or, even before that, to believe in the right way.

—from *A Testament to Freedom* 426

The Easy Yoke

If through our disobedience we evade the gracious Word of God, it becomes a harsh law for us. What is a gentle and easy yoke when done in obedience becomes an insupportable burden when done in disobedience. The more we have hardened ourselves in disobedience against the gracious Word, the harder it is to change, the more obstinately we rebel against God's claim. But just as in our personal life there is only one way, the way of repentance, of patience under God's Word, in which God restores to us our lost communion, so too it is in the church struggle. Without penitence, i.e., unless the church struggle itself becomes our penitence, we shall never receive back the gift we have lost, the church struggle as gospel. Even if the obedience of penitence is harder now than it was then, because we are hardened in our guilt—it is the only way by which God will help us back to the right road.

—from *A Testament to Freedom* 440

Nothing New

We then speak as though we no longer had "a proper joy and certainty" about this way, or, still worse, as though God and God's Word were no longer as clearly present with us as they used to be. In all this, we are ultimately trying to get round what the New Testament calls "patience" and "testing." Paul, at any rate, did not begin to reflect whether his way was the right one when opposition and suffering threatened, nor did Luther. They were both quite certain and glad that they should remain disciples and followers of their Lord. Dear brethren, our real trouble is not doubt about the way upon which we have set out, but our failure to be patient, to keep quiet. We still cannot imagine that today God really doesn't want anything new from us, but simply to prove us in the old way. That is too petty, too monotonous, too undemanding for us. And we simply cannot be constant with the fact that God's cause is not always the successful one, that we really could be "unsuccessful" and yet be on the right road. But this is where we find out whether we have begun in faith or in a burst of enthusiasm.

—from *A Testament to Freedom* 443

Dwelling on God's Word

It is not necessary for us to find new ideas in our meditation. Often that only distracts us and satisfies our vanity. It is perfectly sufficient if the Word enters in and dwells within us as we read and understand it. As Mary "pondered . . . in her heart" what the shepherds told her (Luke 2:19), as a person's words often stick in our mind for a long time—as they dwell and work within us, preoccupy us, disturb us, or make us happy without our being able to do anything about it—so as we meditate, God's Word desires to enter in and stay with us. It desires to move us, to work in us, and to make such an impression on us that the whole day long we will not get away from it. Then it will do its work in us, often without our being aware of it.

—from *Life Together* 88

Ordinary Meditation

Above all, it is not necessary for us to have any unexpected, extraordinary experiences while meditating. That can happen, but if it does not, this is not a sign that the period of meditation has been unprofitable. Not only at the beginning, but time and again a great inner dryness and lack of concern will make itself felt in us, a listlessness, even an inability to mediate. We must not get stuck in such experiences. Above all, we must not allow them to dissuade us from observing our period of meditation with great patience and fidelity. That is why it is not good for us to take too seriously the many bad experiences we have with ourselves during the time of meditation. It is here that our old vanity and the wrongful demands we make on God could sneak into our lives in a pious, roundabout way, as if it were our right to have nothing but edifying and blissful experiences, and as if the discovery of our inner poverty were beneath our dignity. But we will not make any headway with such an attitude.

—from *Life Together* 88

The Word Alone

Impatience and self-reproach only foster our complacency and entangle us ever more deeply in the net of self-centered introspection. But there is no more time to observe ourselves in meditation than there is in the Christian life as a whole. We should pay attention to the Word alone and leave it to the Word to deal effectively with everything. For may it not be the case that it is none other than God who sends us these hours of emptiness and dryness, so that we might once again expect everything from God's Word? "Seek God, not happiness"—that is the fundamental rule of all meditation. If you seek God alone, you will gain happiness—that is the promise of all meditation.

—from *Life Together* 88–89

Time for Silence

Just as there are certain times in a Christian's day for speaking the Word, particularly the time of daily worship and prayer together, so the day also needs certain times of silence under the Word and silence that comes out of the Word. These will mainly be the times before and after hearing the Word. The Word comes not to the noisemakers but to those who are silent. The stillness of the temple is the sign of God's holy presence in the Word. There is an indifferent or even negative attitude toward silence which sees in it a disparagement of God's revelation in the Word. Silence is misunderstood as a solemn gesture, as a mystical desire to get beyond the Word. Silence is no longer seen in its essential relationship to the Word, as the simple act of the individual who falls silent under the Word of God. We are silent before hearing the Word because our thoughts are already focused on the Word, as children are quiet when they enter their father's room. We are silent after hearing the Word because the Word is still speaking and living and dwelling within us. We are silent early in the morning because God should have the first word, and we are silent before going to bed because the last word also belongs to God. We remain silent solely for the sake of the Word, not thereby to dishonor the Word but rather to honor and receive it properly.

—from *Life Together* 84–85

Waiting for God

In the end, silence means nothing other than waiting for God's Word and coming from God's Word with a blessing. But everybody knows this is something that needs to be learned in these days when idle talk has gained the upper hand. Real silence, real stillness, really holding one's tongue, comes only as the sober consequence of spiritual silence. This silence before the Word, however, will have an impact on the whole day. If we have learned to be silent before the Word, we will also learn to manage our silence and our speech during the day. Silence can be forbidden, self-satisfied, haughty, or insulting. From this it follows that silence in itself can never be the issue. The silence of the Christian is listening silence, humble stillness that may be broken at any time for the sake of humility. It is silence in conjunction with the Word. This is what Thomas à Kempis meant when he said: "No one speaks more confidently than the one who gladly remains silent." There is a wonderful power in being silent—the power of clarification, purification, and focus on what is essential. This is true even when considered from a purely profane point of view. But silence before the Word leads to proper hearing and thus also to proper speaking of God's Word at the right time. Much that is unnecessary remains unsaid. But what is essential and helpful can be said in a few words.

—from *Life Together* 85

The Invitation

"Come to me, all you who are weary and burdened, and I will give you rest. Take my yoke upon you and learn from me, for I am gentle and humble in heart, and you will find rest for your souls, for my yoke is easy and my burden is light" (Matt. 11:28–30). Since Jesus spoke these words, there should be no person on earth who feels so abandoned that they could say of themselves: "No one has asked about me. No one has wanted me. No one has ever offered me help." Whoever have once heard these words in their life and speak like this are lying. Indeed, such persons despise and mock Jesus Christ and the seriousness of his words. For he has called all his people who are weary and burdened. He has not made his circle narrow. He has not gathered around himself a spiritual-religious aristocracy. Rather he has made the circle as wide as possible, so wide that actually not a single person could say in good conscience that Jesus's invitation was not meant for him or her because they were not among the weary and burdened. On the contrary, what is so astonishing about this invitation is that it actually puts all people in the awkward position of having to admit that Jesus's invitation was meant for them too. In fact, perhaps for them even more than for others.

—from *A Testament to Freedom* 234

Who Is Weary?

There is hardly anything more depressing for us than when we realize that outwardly we have everything we want, but with all that we have nevertheless remain inwardly hollow and empty and superficial. With all of our possessions we cannot buy the most important things of this earthly life—inner peace, spiritual joy, love in marriage and family. One can see precisely in the homes of apparently successful people just how much unspeakable inward suffering there is and how great a burden of heavy guilt this wealth produces. . . . However even those who seem not even to feel their loneliness, because they are so intoxicated with life as it rushes along day by day, do not even think of being weary and burdened. Yet in reality they too are a part of this group. It is just the reverse. They plunge into their supposed happiness ever more wildly because they do know or suspect at the bottom of their heart that they too are part of it and because they are afraid of admitting that to themselves. They are on the run from every word that might tell them the truth. They do not want to be weary and burdened and yet in the eyes of Christ they are doubly so.

—from *A Testament to Freedom* 235

The Lifted Burden

When we become a burden to ourselves, when we don't want to keep on going, when we are afraid of the mountain lying in front of us, when guilt feelings weigh heavily on our mind, when we feel we have been lied to and victimized by the world, then we need only one thing—we need a person whom we can fully trust without reservation, a person who understands everything, hears everything, a person who bears all things, believes all things, hopes all things, forgives all things. We need a person to whom we can say: "You are rest, you are gentle peace, you are the longing and the one who stills it" (Ruckert). We need a person under whose eyes our suffering disappears and our heart opens up in silent love, a person who gently takes our burden from us and frees us from our fits of rage and from all our fears. In so doing, this person delivers our soul from this world. . . . Now the greatest of all miracles is that every individual has and can find this person because this person calls each of us to himself on his own initiative, offers himself, invites us. This person who is our rest, our peace, our refreshment, and our deliverance, is Jesus Christ alone. He alone is truly human. And in this true humanity he is God.

—from *A Testament to Freedom* 235–236

Under the Yoke

There are two possible ways to help persons who are oppressed by a burden. Either you take the whole load off of them so that in the future they have nothing more to carry. Or you help them carry it by making the carrying easier for them. Jesus does not want to go the first way with us. The load is not taken from us. Jesus who carried his own cross knows that we are destined to be burden carriers and the bearers of our own cross. Moreover, he knows that we are sanctified only under this burden and not without this burden. Jesus does not take from us the burden God has laid upon us. But he makes the burden easier for us by showing us how we must carry it. . . . A yoke is a burden itself, a burden in addition to all the other burdens; and yet it has a peculiar way of making the other burdens easier. . . . We are well acquainted with the yoke of the draft animals. The yoke alone enables them to pull the heavy burden without feeling pain or torment in the process, and without getting sore skin from pulling it. Jesus wants to put us human beings under such a yoke so that our burden does not become too heavy for us. He calls it "my yoke." It is the yoke under which he learned to carry his burden. His burden is a thousand times heavier than all our burdens precisely because he carries all of our burdens.

—from *A Testament to Freedom* 236

No Easy Cause

In the light of such blessed hope and such deliverance from the troubles and sin and guilt of this life, it may be said even today: "My yoke is easy and my burden is light." Woe to those who play with these words and act as if it meant that Christ's cause is an easy cause. The person who recoils in horror from the seriousness and the frightfulness of this cause of Christ understands much more about these words. The person who really understands it does not dare to approach this cause for fear of what it may mean for our real life. But, of course, then we must say to the one who has once comprehended what Jesus Christ and his will are all about: Now go to Jesus yourself and take his yoke upon yourself and see how everything has suddenly become different and all your fears and all your dismay will vanish. See how all of a sudden it may be said of the one who is with Jesus: "My yoke is easy."

—from *A Testament to Freedom* 237

October

A New Call

When I first began theology, I imagined it to be somewhat different—perhaps more like an academic affair. Now it has become something completely different from that. And now I believe I know at last that I am at least on the right track—for the first time in my life. And that often makes me very glad. I continue to fear only that I might no longer appreciate the genuine anxiety for meaning of other people, but remain set in my ways. I believe I know that inwardly I shall be really clear and honest only when I have begun to take seriously the Sermon on the Mount. Here is set the only source of power capable of exploding the whole enchantment and specter [Hitler and his rule] so that only a few burnt-out fragments are left remaining from the fireworks. The restoration of the church will surely come from a sort of new monasticism which has in common with the old only the uncompromising attitude of a life lived according to the Sermon on the Mount in the following of Christ. I believe it is now time to call people to this.

—from *A Testament to Freedom* 424

Serious Grace

Persons who are puzzled about faith mean to take God seriously when they doubt that God is gracious toward them. But God is not taken seriously when one's own being lost is taken more seriously than the grace of God, which is able to take away and emerge victorious over that lost condition. It is also not taking God seriously when we elevate our concept of God as divine wrath above God's essence, namely the reality of God's grace. God is gracious above and beyond all our sins. Those who want to take God seriously should look upon Christ. In Christ God's wrath is revealed as nowhere else, yet at the same time God's grace is revealed as nowhere else. If you think you are under God's wrath, then cleave to Christ! "For his anger is but for a moment, and his favor is for a lifetime" (Ps. 30:5).

—from *A Testament to Freedom* 181

God's Yes

We are preachers of justification by grace alone. What must that mean today? It means quite simply that we should no longer equate human ways and aims with divine ways and aims. God is beyond all human plans and actions. Everything must be judged by God. Anyone who evades this judgment of God must die, those who subject themselves to it will live; for to be judged by God is grace that leads to life. God judges in order to have mercy and humbles in order to exalt. Only the humble will succeed. God does not confirm human action, but cuts across it, and thereby draws our gaze above, to God's grace. In cutting across our ways, God comes to us and says a gracious "Yes" to us, but only through the cross of Jesus Christ. He has placed this cross upon the earth. Under the cross he returns us to the earth, and its work and toil, but in so doing he binds us anew to the earth and to the people who live, act, fight, and suffer upon it. "You then, my child, be strong in the grace that is in Christ Jesus" (2 Tim. 2:1), "Be strong, be courageous, and keep the charge of the Lord your God" (1 Kings 2:2ff).

—from *A Testament to Freedom* 446

Where Is God?

"Your steadfast love is better than life" (Ps. 63:3). Two and a half millennia have now passed since the ancient Jewish saint, far from Jerusalem and his homeland, devoured by misery in body and soul, surrounded by mockers and enemies of his God, pondered the strange and wonderful ways God had led him. It was no easy, peaceful meditation. It was a struggle for God and God's faithfulness. The pillars of life had crumbled away. Where his hand thought it had found firm support it reached into an empty nothingness. "God, where are you? God, who am I? My life falls crashing down into the bottomless abyss. God, I am afraid, where has your goodness gone? And yet, you are my God and your goodness is better than life." That is one of the words that does not let you go once you have understood it, a word that seems to shine gently, but is inwardly hard, a word of passion that is engendered where two worlds clash, that is, a word from the world of the Bible and not from our own.

—from *A Testament to Freedom* 194

God's Favorites

What if, precisely at the moment when we are thanking God for God's goodness toward us, there is a ring at the door, as so often happens these days, and we find someone standing there who also would like to thank God for some small gift, but to whom such a gift has been denied and who is starving with starving children and who will go to bed in bitterness? What becomes of our grace in such moments? Will we really feel like saying that God is merciful to *us* and angry with *them*, or that the fact that we still have something to eat proves that we have won a special position of favor in God's sight, that God feeds the favorite children and lets the unworthy go hungry? May the merciful God protect us from the temptation of such gratitude. May God lead us to a true understanding of God's goodness. . . . If we want to understand God's goodness in God's gifts, then we must think of them as a responsibility we bear for our brothers and sisters. Let none say: God has blessed us with money and possessions, and then live as if they and their God were alone in the world. For the time will come when they realize that they have been worshipping the idols of their good fortune and selfishness. Possessions are not God's blessing and goodness, but the opportunities of service which God entrusts to us.

—from *A Testament to Freedom* 196–197

God in Our Guilt

But now comes the greatest wonder that the world has ever known. In the very place where we have fallen away from God, where we have become dead and unreceptive to God, in our guilt, God's goodness searches us out, and is revealed to us again as *the* eternal promise of God, in Jesus Christ, which far surpasses all guilt and all life. Only the person who, in the darkness of guilt, of unfaithfulness, of enmity toward God, has felt himself or herself touched by the love which never ceases, which forgives everything, and which points beyond all misery to the world of God, only such a person really knows what God's goodness means.

—from *A Testament to Freedom* 198

The Kingdom of Peace

God's way in the world leads to the cross and through the cross to life. Therefore, do not be afraid; fear not; be faithful! But what is meant here by being faithful is namely: to stand and to fall with the Word of Christ, with his sermon about the kingdom of peace, to know that the Words of Christ in spite of all are mightier than the powers of evil. What is meant here by being faithful as a congregation of Christ is namely: to be in this furious storm even to exhaustion, even to vexation, even to the call to martyrdom for the Word of Christ, so that there will be peace, so that there will be love, so that there will be salvation, and so that he is our peace and that God is a God of peace.

—from *A Testament to Freedom* 203

The Privilege of Community

The Christian cannot simply take for granted the privilege of living among other Christians. Jesus Christ lived in the midst of his enemies. In the end all his disciples abandoned him. On the cross he was all alone, surrounded by criminals and the jeering crowds. He had come for the express purpose of bringing peace to the enemies of God. So Christians, too, belong not in the seclusion of a cloistered life but in the midst of enemies. There they find their mission, their work. "To rule is to be in the midst of your enemies. And whoever will not suffer this does not want to be part of the rule of Christ; such a person wants to be among friends and sit among the roses and lilies, not with the bad people but the religious people. O you blasphemers and betrayers of Christ! If Christ had done what you are doing, who would ever have been saved?" (Luther). "Though I scattered them among the nations, yet in far countries they shall remember me" (Zech. 10:9). According to God's will, the Christian church is a scattered people, scattered like seed "to all the kingdoms of the earth" (Deut. 28:25). That is the curse and its promise. God's people must live in distant lands among the unbelievers, but they will be the seed of the kingdom of God in all the world.

—from *Life Together* 27–28

The Promised Community

Thus in the period between the death of Christ and the day of judgment, when Christians are allowed to live here in visible community with other Christians, we have merely a gracious anticipation of the end time. It is by God's grace that a congregation is permitted to gather visibly around God's word and sacrament in this world. Not all Christians partake of this grace. The imprisoned, the sick, the lonely who live in the diaspora, the proclaimers of the gospel in heathen lands stand alone. They know that the visible community is grace. They pray with the psalmist: "I went with the throng, and led them in procession to the house of God, with glad shouts and songs of thanksgiving, a multitude keeping festival" (Ps. 42:5). But they remain alone in distant lands, a scattered seed according to God's will. Yet what is denied them as a visible experience they grasp more ardently in faith. Hence "in the Spirit on the Lord's Day" (Rev. 1:10) the exiled disciple of the Lord, John the author of the Apocalypse, celebrates the worship of heaven with its congregations in the loneliness of the Island of Patmos. He sees the seven lampstands that are the congregations, the seven stars that are the angels of the congregations, and in the midst and above it all, the Son of Man, Jesus Christ, in his great glory as the risen one. He strengthens and comforts John by his word. That is the heavenly community in which the exile participates on the day of his Lord's resurrection.

—from *Life Together* 28–29

Good Company

The physical presence of other Christians is a source of incomparable joy and strength to the believer. With great yearning the imprisoned apostle Paul calls his "beloved son in the faith," Timothy, to come to him in prison in the last days of his life (1 Tim. 1:2). He wants to see him again and have him near. Paul has not forgotten the tears Timothy shed during their final parting (2 Tim. 1:4). Thinking of the congregation in Thessalonica, Paul prays "night and day . . . most earnestly that we may see you face to face" (1 Thess. 3:10). The aged John knows his joy in his own people will only be complete when he can come to them and speak to them face to face instead of using paper and ink (2 John 12). The believer need not feel any shame when yearning for the physical presence of other Christians, as if one were still living too much in the flesh. A human being is created as a body; the Son of God appeared on earth in the body for our sake and was raised in the body. In the sacrament the believer receives the Lord Christ in the body, and the resurrection of the dead will bring about the perfected community of God's spiritual-physical creatures. Therefore, the believer praises the Creator, the Reconciler, and the Redeemer, God the Father, Son and Holy Spirit, for the bodily presence of the other Christian.

—from *Life Together* 29

Meeting God

The prisoner, the sick person, the Christian living in the diaspora recognizes in the nearness of a fellow Christian a physical sign of the gracious presence of the triune God. In their loneliness, both the visitor and the one visited recognize in each other the Christ who is present in the body. They receive and meet each other as one meets the Lord, in reverence, humility, and joy. They receive each other's blessings as the blessing of the Lord Jesus Christ. But if there is so much happiness and joy even in a single encounter of one Christian with another, what inexhaustible riches must invariably open up for those who by God's will are privileged to live in daily community life with other Christians! Of course, what is an inexpressible blessing from God for the lonely individual is easily disregarded and trampled under foot by those who receive the gift every day. It is easily forgotten that the community of Christians is a gift of grace from the kingdom of God, a gift that can be taken from us any day—that the time still separating us from the most profound loneliness may be brief indeed. Therefore, let those who until now have had the privilege of living a Christian life together with other Christians praise God's grace from the bottom of their hearts. Let them thank God on their knees and realize: it is grace, nothing but grace, that we are still permitted to live in the community of Christians today.

—from *Life Together* 29

Loneliness

Many persons seek community because they are afraid of loneliness. Because they can no longer endure being alone, such people are driven to seek the company of others. Christians, too, who cannot cope on their own, and who in their own lives have had some bad experiences, hope to experience help with this in the company of other people. More often than not, they are disappointed. They then blame the community for what is really their own fault. The Christian community is not a spiritual sanatorium. Those who take refuge in community while fleeing from themselves are misusing it to indulge in empty talk and distraction, no matter how spiritual this idle talk and distraction may appear. In reality they are not seeking community at all, but only a thrill that will allow them to forget their isolation for a short time. It is precisely such misuse of community that creates the deadly isolation of human beings. Such attempts to find healing result in the undermining of speech and all genuine experience and, finally, resignation and spiritual death.

—from *Life Together* 81–82

Being Alone

Whoever cannot be alone should beware of community. Such people will only do harm to themselves and to the community. Alone you stood before God when God called you. Alone you had to obey God's voice. Alone you had to take up your cross, struggle, and pray, and alone you will die and give an account to God. You cannot avoid yourself, for it is precisely God who has singled you out. If you do not want to be alone, you are rejecting Christ's call to you, and you can have no part in the community of those who are called. "The confrontation with death and its demands comes to us all; no one can die for another. All must fight their own battle with death by themselves, alone. I will not be with you then, nor you with me" (Luther).

—from *Life Together* 82

Living In Community

Whoever cannot stand being in community should beware of being alone. You are called into the community of faith; the call was not meant for you alone. You carry your cross, you struggle, and you pray in the community of faith, the community of those who are called. You are not alone even when you die, and on the day of judgment you will be only one member of the great community of faith in Jesus Christ. If you neglect the community of other Christians, you reject the call of Jesus Christ, and thus your being alone can only become harmful for you. "If I die, then I am not alone in death; if I suffer, they (the community of faith) suffer with me" (Luther). We recognize, then, that only as we stand within the community can we be alone, and only those who are alone can life in the community. Both belong together. Only in the community do we learn to be properly alone; and only in being alone do we learn to live properly in the community. It is not as if the one preceded the other; rather that both begin at the same time, namely, with the call of Jesus Christ.

—from *Life Together* 82–83

Community and Solitude

Those who want community without solitude plunge into the void of words and feelings, and those who seek solitude without community perish in the bottomless pit of vanity, self-infatuation, and despair. Whoever cannot be alone should beware of community. Whoever cannot stand being in community should beware of being alone. The day together of Christians who live in community is accompanied by each individual's day alone. That is the way it must be. The day together will be unfruitful without the day alone, both for the community and for the individual. The mark of solitude is silence, just as speech is the mark of community. Silence and speech have the same inner connection and distinction as do being alone and community. One does not exist without the other. Genuine speech comes out of silence, and genuine silence comes out of speech.

—from *Life Together* 83

Will for the Future

The essence of optimism is not its view of the present, but the fact that it is the inspiration of life and hope when others give in; it enables people to hold their heads high when everything seems to be going wrong; it gives them strength to sustain reverses and yet to claim the future for themselves instead of abandoning it to their opponents. It is true that there is a silly, cowardly kind of optimism, which we must condemn. But the optimism that is will for the future should never be despised, even if it is proven wrong a hundred times; it is health and vitality, and the sick person has no business to impugn it. There are people who regard it as frivolous, and some Christians think it impious for anyone to hope and prepare for a better earthly future. They think that the meaning of present events is chaos, disorder, and catastrophe; and in resignation or pious escapism they surrender all responsibility for reconstruction and for future generations. It may be that the day of judgment will dawn tomorrow; and in that case, though not before, we shall gladly stop working for a better future.

—from *Letters and Papers from Prison* 16

Wholesome Reserve

Unless we have the courage to fight for a revival of wholesome reserve between people, we shall perish in an anarchy of human values. The impudent contempt for such reserve is the mark of the rabble, just as inward uncertainty, haggling, and cringing for the favor of insolent people, and lowering oneself to the level of the rabble are the way of becoming no better than the rabble itself. When we forget what is due to ourselves and to others, when the feeling for human quality and the power to exercise reserve cease to exist, chaos is at the door. When we tolerate impudence for the sake of material comforts, then we abandon our self-respect; the floodgates are opened, chaos bursts the dam that we were to defend; and we are responsible for it all.

—from *Letters and Papers from Prison* 12

Sin Boldly

Luther's statement, ["Sin boldly"], is to be understood correctly not as a beginning, but exclusively as an end, a conclusion, a last stone, as the very last word. Understood as a presupposition, *pecca fortiter* (sin boldly) becomes an ethical principle. If grace is a principle, then pecca fortiter as a principle would correspond to it. That is justification of sin. It turns Luther's statement into its opposite. "Sin boldly"—that could be for Luther only the very last bit of pastoral advice, of consolation for those who along the path of discipleship have come to know that they cannot become sin-free, who out of fear of sin despair of God's grace. For them, "sin boldly" is not something like a fundamental affirmation of their disobedient lives. Rather, it is the gospel of God's grace, in the presence of which we are sinners always and at every place.

—from *Discipleship* 52

Believe Boldly

[The] gospel seeks us and justifies us exactly as sinners. Admit your sin boldly; do not try to flee from it, but "believe much more boldly." You are a sinner, so just be a sinner. Do not want to be anything else than what you are. Become a sinner again every day and be bold in doing so. But to whom could such a thing be said except to those who from their hearts daily reject sin, who every day reject everything that hinders them from following Jesus and who are still unconsoled about their daily unfaithfulness and sin? Who else could hear it without danger for their faith than those who are called anew by such consolation to follow Christ? In this way, Luther's statement, understood as a conclusion, becomes that costly grace which alone is grace.

—from *Discipleship* 52–53

Tactless Truth

The Day of Repentance is the day in which we are reminded through a word of the Bible . . . that the end will bring a complete uncovering, a complete exposure of our whole life. "We must all appear before the judgment seat of Christ" (2 Cor. 5:10). This goes against a human being's inner nature. We have something to hide. We have secrets, worries, thoughts, hopes, desires, passions which no one else gets to know. We are sensitive when people get near such domains with their questions. And now, against all rules of tact the Bible speaks of the truth that in the end we will appear before Christ with everything we are and were; and not only before Christ, but also before the people who will stand next to us. And we all know, that we could justify ourselves before any human court, but not before this one. Lord, who can justify themselves?

—from *A Testament to Freedom* 217

Christ Our Judge

Christ will judge. His Spirit will separate those of different opinion. He who was poor and weak among us, will in the end pass judgment on all the world. There is only one question which is important: What do you think about this spirit, what do you think about this man Jesus Christ? It is possible to take different positions on every other Spirit, on every other person. The ultimate is not subject to such positions. In the face of Christ, there is only a straight "Yes" or a straight "No" because he is the spirit, by which every human spirit must be judged. None can escape and none can bypass him—even if they think they can, if they frivolously and carelessly think they can stand on their own and be their own judge. None are their own judge. Christ is the judge of humankind. His judgment is eternal. Those who pass him by without having clearly said his "Yes" or "No" will have to stand opposite him and look him in the face in the hour of death when their lives are weighed in eternity. And his question will be: "Have you lived a life of love toward God and humans, or have you lived for yourself?" Here there is no more subterfuge, no excuses, no beating around the bush; here one's whole life lies open before the light of Christ.

—from *A Testament to Freedom* 217–218

The Path to Christ

The Bible does not really want to frighten us. God does not want people to be afraid. Not even at the last judgment. But God lets us know so that we may perceive what life is. God lets it be known today so that we may lead a life in openness and in the light of the last judgment. God lets us know—only so that we find the path to Jesus Christ, so that we may turn from our evil way and meet him. God does not want to frighten people; God sends us the word about judgment so that we may all the more passionately, all the more eagerly, seize the promise of grace, so that we recognize that we do not stand before God in our own strength, lest we should perish before God; that in spite of everything God does not desire our death, but rather our life.

—from *A Testament to Freedom* 218

The Compassionate Judge

Christ judges. It is truly serious. But it also means: the Compassionate One judges, he who lived among tax collectors and sinners, who was tempted even as we are, who carried and endured in his own body our sufferings, our fears, our desires, who knows us and calls us by name. Christ judges; that means, grace is the judge, forgiveness, and love. Whoever clings to these is already acquitted. Of course whoever refer to their own work Christ will judge and condemn according to these works. But we should have joy on that day; we should not tremble and lose heart, but gladly entrust ourselves into his hand. . . . Come, judgment day—joyfully we wait for you, since we shall see the merciful Lord and take his hand and he will love us.

—from *A Testament to Freedom* 218

The Heritage of the Future

The West is about to repudiate its historical heritage. It is becoming hostile to Christ. This is the unique situation of our time, and it is actual decay. The Christian churches stand in the middle of the dissolution of all that exists, as protectors of the heritage of the Middle Ages and the Reformation, but above all as witnesses to the miracle of God in Jesus Christ "yesterday, today, and forever" (Heb. 13:8). Next to the churches, however, stands "the restraining power," the remnant of ordering power, that still effectively resists decay. The church has a unique task. The *corpus christianum* has broken apart. The *corpus* Christi stands over against a hostile world. The church must bear witness to Jesus Christ as living lord, and it must do so in a world that has turned away from Christ after knowing him. As bearer of a historical heritage, the church, while waiting for Judgment Day, has an obligation to the historical future. Its vision of the end of all things must not paralyze its historical responsibility. The church must leave the end to God as well as the possibility that history will continue. Both remain its concern.

—from *Ethics* 132

The Living Lord

In sticking to its calling—that is, preaching the risen Jesus Christ—the church deals a deadly blow to the spirit of annihilation. The "restraining power," the ordering force, however, sees the church as an ally; and all the elements of order that still remain seek to be near the church. Justice, truth, science, art, culture, humanity, freedom, and patriotism, after long wanderings, find their way back to their origin. The more the church holds to its central message, the more effective it is. Its suffering is infinitely more dangerous to the spirit of destruction than the political power that it may still retain. The church makes clear with its message of the living Lord Jesus Christ, however, that it is not simply concerned with preserving what has been handed down from the past. It forces the custodians of power in particular to listen and change their ways. But it does not push away those who come to it and seek to be near it. The church leaves to God's rule of the world whether God will allow the custodians of power to succeed, and whether the church—preserving its difference and yet joining in sincere alliance with those powers—may pass on to the future the historical heritage, laden with the blessing and guilt of the forebears.

—from *Ethics* 132–133

The Failure of Reason

The failure of *reasonable people* is appalling; they cannot manage to see either the abyss of evil or the abyss of holiness. With the best intentions they believe that, with a little reason, they can pull back together a structure that has come apart at the joints. In their defective vision they want to be fair to both sides, and so they are crushed between the colliding forces without having accomplished anything at all. Bitterly disappointed that the world is so unreasonable, they see themselves condemned to ineffectiveness. They withdraw in resignation or fall helplessly captive to the stronger party. More appalling is the bankruptcy of all ethical *fanaticism*. Fanatics believe that they can face the power of evil with the purity of their will and their principles. But the essence of fanaticism is that it loses sight of the whole evil, and like a bull that charges the red cape instead of the one holding it, fanatics finally tire and suffer defeat. Fanatics miss their goal. Though their fanaticism serves the lofty goals of truth or justice, sooner or later they are caught in small and insignificant things and fall into the net of their more clever opponent.

—from *Ethics* 78

Dangerous Folly

Folly is a more dangerous enemy to the good than evil. One can protest against evil; it can be unmasked and, if need be, prevented by force. Evil always carries the seeds of its own destruction, as it makes people, at the least, uncomfortable. Against folly we have no defence. Neither protests nor force can touch it; reasoning is no use; facts that contradict personal prejudices can simply be disbelieved—indeed, the fool can counter by criticizing them, and if they are undeniable, they can just be pushed aside as trivial exceptions. So the fool, as distinct from the scoundrel, is completely self-satisfied; in fact, he can easily become dangerous, as it does not take much to make him aggressive. A fool must therefore be treated more cautiously than a scoundrel; we shall never again try to convince a fool by reason, for it is both useless and dangerous.

—from *Letters and Papers from Prison* 7

The Nature of Foolishness

If we are to deal adequately with folly, we must try to understand its nature. This much is certain, that it is a moral rather than an intellectual defect. There are people who are mentally agile but foolish, and people who are mentally slow but very far from foolish—a discovery that we make to our surprise as a result of particular situations. We thus get the impression that folly is likely to be not a congenital defect, but one that is acquired in certain circumstances where people make fools of themselves or allow others to make fools of them. We notice further that this defect is less common in the unsociable and solitary than in individuals or groups that are inclined or condemned to sociability. It seems, then, that folly is a sociological rather than a psychological problem, and that it is a special form of the operation of historical circumstances on people, a psychological by-product of definite external factors. If we look more closely, we see that any violent display of power, whether political or religious, produces an outburst of folly in a large part of humanity; indeed this seems actually to be a psychological and sociological law: the power of some needs the folly of others.

—from *Letters and Papers from Prison* 7–8

The Stubborn Fool

The upsurge of power makes such an overwhelming impression that people are deprived of their independent judgment, and—more or less unconsciously—give up trying to assess a new state of affairs for themselves. The fact that the fool is often stubborn must not mislead us into thinking that he is independent. One feels in fact, when talking to him, that one is dealing, not with the man himself, but with slogans, catchwords, and the like, which have taken hold of him. He is under the spell, he is blinded, his very nature is being misused and exploited. Having thus become a passive instrument, the fool will be capable of any evil and at the same time incapable of seeing that it is evil. Here lies the danger of a diabolical exploitation that can do irreparable damage to human beings.

—from *Letters and Papers from Prison* 8

Defeating Folly

Folly can be overcome, not by instruction, but only by an act of liberation; and so we have to come to terms with the fact that in the great majority of cases inward liberation must be preceded by outward liberation, and that until that has taken place, we may as well abandon all attempts to convince the fool. In this state of affairs we have to realize why it is no use our trying to find out what "the people" really think, and why the question is so superfluous for the person who thinks and acts responsibly—but always given these particular circumstances. The Bible's words that "the fear of the Lord is the beginning of wisdom" (Ps. 111:10) tell us that a person's inward liberation to live a responsible life before God is the only real cure for folly. But there is some consolation in these thoughts on folly: they in no way justify our thinking that most people are fools in all circumstances. What will really matter is whether those in power expect more from people's folly than from their wisdom and independence of mind.

—from *Letters and Papers from Prison* 8–9

Unintended Consequences

Today is Reformation Day, a feast that in our time can give one plenty to think about. One wonders why Luther's action had to be followed by consequences that were the exact opposite of what he intended and that darkened the last years of his life, so he sometimes even doubted the value of his life's work. He wanted a real unity of the Church and the West—that is, of the Christian peoples, and the consequence was the disintegration of the Church and of Europe; he wanted the "freedom of the Christian man," and the consequence was indifference and licentiousness; he wanted the establishment of a genuine secular social order free from clerical privilege, and the result was insurrection, the Peasants' War, and soon afterward the gradual dissolution of all real cohesion and order in society. I remember from my student days a discussion between Holl and Harnack as to whether the great historical intellectual and spiritual movements made headway through their primary of their secondary motives. At the time I thought Holl was right in maintaining the former; now I think he was wrong. As long as a hundred years ago Kierkegaard said that today Luther would say the opposite of what he said then. I think he was right—with some reservations.

—from *Letters and Papers from Prison* 51–52

November

Idolizing Success

Where the figure of a successful person becomes especially prominent, the majority fall into idolizing success. They become blind to right and wrong, truth and lie, decency and malice. They see only the deed, the success. Ethical and intellectual capacity for judgment grow dull before the sheen of success and before the desire somehow to share in it. People even fail to perceive that guilt is scarred over in success, because guilt is no longer recognized as such. Success per se is the good. This attitude is only genuine and excusable while one is intoxicated by events. After sobriety returns it can be maintained only at the cost of deep inner hypocrisy, with conscious self-deception. This leads to an inner depravity, from which recovery is difficult.

—from *Ethics* 89

The Good and the Successful

The statement that success is the good is challenged by an opposing one that looks at the conditions of lasting success, namely, that only the good is successful. Here the capacity for judgment is retained in the face of success. Here right remains right and wrong remains wrong. Here one does not close one's eyes at the decisive moment, only to open them again after the deed has been done. And here, consciously or unconsciously, a law of the world is acknowledged according to which justice, truth, and order are, in the long view, more stable than violence, lies, and arbitrariness. Still, this optimistic thesis leads one astray. Either historical facts must be falsified in order to demonstrate the unsuccessfulness of evil, which will lead quickly again to the reverse proposition that success is the good, or optimism collapses in the face of the facts and ends by denouncing all historical success.

—from *Ethics* 89–90

Disarming Success

The form of the crucified disarms all thinking aimed at success, for it is a denial of judgment. Neither the triumph of the successful, nor bitter hatred of the successful by those who fail, can finally cope with the world. Jesus is certainly no advocate for the successful in history, but neither does he lead the revolt of the failures against the successful. His concern is neither success nor failure but willing acceptance of the judgment of God. Only in judgment is there reconciliation with God and among human beings. Christ sets the human person judged by God, the successful and the unsuccessful, over against all thinking that revolves around success or failure. God judges people because, out of sheer love, God wants them to be able to stand before God. It is a judgment of grace that God in Christ brings on human beings. Over against the successful, God sanctifies pain, lowliness, failure, poverty, loneliness, and despair in the cross of Christ. . . . The Yes of God to the cross is judgment on the successful. But the unsuccessful must realize that it is not their lack of success, not their place as pariahs as such, that lets them stand before God, but only their acceptance of the judgment of divine love. It is a mystery of God's reign over the world that this very cross, the sign of Christ's failure in the world, can in turn lead to historical success.

—from *Ethics* 90–91

Interrupted by God

We must be ready to allow ourselves to be interrupted by God, who will thwart our plans and frustrate our ways time and again, even daily, by sending people across our path with their demands and requests. We can, then, pass them by, preoccupied with our more important daily tasks, just as the priest—perhaps reading the Bible—passed by the man who had fallen among robbers (Luke 10:31). When we do that, we pass by the visible sign of the cross raised in our lives to show us that God's way, and not our own, is what counts. It is a strange fact that, of all people, Christians and theologians often consider their work so important and urgent that they do not want to let anything interrupt it. They think they are doing God a favor, but actually they are despising God's "crooked yet straight path" (Gottfried Arnold). They want to know nothing about how human plans are thwarted. But it is part of the school of humility that we must not spare our hand where it can perform a service. We do not manage our time ourselves but allow it to be occupied by God.

—from *Life Together* 99–100

Two Realms

This division of the whole of reality into sacred and profane, or Christian and worldly, sectors creates the possibility of existence in only one of these sectors: for instance, a spiritual existence that takes no part in worldly existence, and a worldly existence that can make good its claim to autonomy over against the sacred sector. The monk and the cultural Protestant of the nineteenth century represent these two possibilities. The whole of medieval history turned around the theme of the rule of the spiritual realm over the worldly, the realm of grace over the realm of nature, whereas the modern age is characterized by an ever-progressing independence of the worldly over against the spiritual. As long as Christ and the world are conceived as two realms bumping against and repelling each other, we are left with only the following options. Giving up on reality as a whole, either we place ourselves in one of the two realms, wanting Christ without the world or the world without Christ—and in both cases we deceive ourselves. Or we try to stand in the two realms at the same time, thereby becoming people in eternal conflict, shaped by the post-Reformation era, who ever and again present ourselves as the *only* form of Christian existence that is in accord with reality.

—from *Ethics* 57–58

Community through Christ

Christian community means community through Jesus Christ and in Jesus Christ. There is no Christian community that is more than this, and none that is less that this. Whether it be a brief, single encounter or the daily community of many years, Christian community is solely this: we belong to one another only through and in Jesus Christ. What does this mean? It means, *first,* that a Christian needs others for the sake of Jesus Christ. It means, *second*, that a Christian comes to others only through Jesus Christ. It means, *third*, that from eternity we have been chosen in Jesus Christ, accepted in time, and united for eternity. . . . Christians live entirely by the truth of God's word in Jesus Christ. . . . But God put this Word into the mouth of human beings so that it may be passed on to others. When people are deeply affected by the Word, they tell it to other people. God has willed that we should seek and find God's living Word in the testimony of other Christians, in the mouths of human beings. Therefore, Christians need other Christians to speak God's word to them. They need them again and again when they become uncertain and disheartened because, living by their own resources, they cannot help themselves without cheating themselves out of the truth. They need other Christians as bearers and proclaimers of the divine word of salvation. They need them solely for the sake of Jesus Christ.

—from *Life Together* 31–32

Bound Together

Without Christ we would not know God; we could neither call on God nor come to God. Moreover, without Christ we would not know other Christians around us; nor could we approach them. The way to them is blocked by one's own ego. Christ opened up the way to God and to one another. Now Christians, can live with each other in peace; they can love and serve one another; they can become one. But they can continue to do so only through Jesus Christ. Only in Jesus Christ are we one; only through him are we bound together. He remains the one and only mediator throughout eternity.

—from *Life Together* 33

We Are in Christ

When God's Son took on flesh, he truly and bodily, out of pure grace, took on our being, our nature, ourselves. This was the eternal decree of the triune God. Now we are in him. Wherever he is, he bears our flesh, he bears us. And, where he is, there we are too—in the incarnation, on the cross, and in his resurrection. We belong to him because we are in him. That is why the Scriptures call us the body of Christ. But if we have been elected and accepted with the whole church in Jesus Christ before we could know it or want it, then we also belong to Christ in eternity with one another. We who live here in community with Christ will one day be with Christ in eternal community. Those who look at other Christians should know that they will be eternally united with them in Jesus Christ. Christian community means community through and in Jesus Christ. Everything the Scriptures provide in the way of directions and rules for Christians' life together rests on this presupposition.

—from *Life Together* 33

Spiritual Community

The basis of all pneumatic, or spiritual, reality is the clear, manifest Word of God in Jesus Christ. At the foundation of all psychic, or emotional, reality are the dark, impenetrable urges and desires of the human soul. The basis of spiritual community is truth; the basis of emotional community is desire. The essence of spiritual community is light. For "God is light and in [God] there is no darkness at all" (1 John 1:5); and "if we walk in the light as he himself is in the light, we have fellowship with one another" (1 John 1:7). The essence of emotional, self-centered community is darkness, "for it is from within, from the human heart, that evil intentions come" (Mark 7:21). It is the deep night that spreads over the sources of all human activity, over even all noble and devout impulses. Spiritual community is the community of those who are called by Christ; emotional community is the community of pious souls. The bright love of Christian service, *agape*, lives in the spiritual community; the dark love of pious-impious urges, *eros*, burns in the self-centered community. In the former, there is ordered, Christian service; in the latter, disordered desire for pleasure. In the former, there is humble submission of Christians one to another; in the later, humble, yet haughty subjection of other Christians to one's own desires.

—from *Life Together* 39–40

Ruled by the Spirit

In the spiritual community the Word of God alone rules; in the emotional, self-centered community the individual who is equipped with exceptional powers, experience, and magical, suggestive abilities rules along with the Word. In the one, God's Word alone is binding; in the other, besides the Word, human beings bind others to themselves. In the one, all power, honor, and rule are surrendered to the Holy Spirit; in the other, power and personal spheres of influence are sought and cultivated. So far as these are devout people, they certainly seek this power with the intention of serving the highest and the best. But in reality they end up dethroning the Holy Spirit and banishing it to the realm of unreal remoteness; only what is self-centered remains real here. Thus, in the spiritual community the Spirit rules; in the emotional community, psychological techniques and methods. In the former, unsophisticated, nonpsychological, unmethodical, helping love is offered to one another; in the latter, psychological analysis and design. In the former, service to one another is simple and humble; in the latter, it is to strangers treated in a searching, calculating fashion.

—from *Life Together* 40

False Relationship

Within the spiritual community there is never, in any way whatsoever, an "immediate" relationship of one to another. However, in the self-centered community there exists a profound, elemental emotional desire for community, for immediate contact with other human souls, just as in the flesh there is a yearning for immediate union with other flesh. This desire of the human soul seeks the complete intimate fusion of I and You, whether this occurs in the union of love or—what from this self-centered perspective is after all the same thing—in forcing the other into one's own sphere of power and influence. Here is where self-centered, strong people enjoy life to the full, securing for themselves the admiration, the love, or the fear of the weak. Here human bonds, suggestive influences, and dependencies are everything.

—from *Life Together* 41

Self-Centered Love

There is . . . a "merely emotional" love of neighbor. Such love is capable of making the most unheard-of sacrifices. Often it far surpasses the genuine love of Christ in fervent devotion and visible results. It speaks the Christian language with overwhelming and stirring eloquence. But it is what the apostle Paul is speaking of when he says: "If I give all I possess to the poor, and surrender my body to the flames" (1 Cor. 13:3)—in other words, if I combine the utmost deeds of love with the utmost of devotion—"but do not have love (that is, the love of Christ), I would be nothing" (1 Cor. 13:2). Self-centered love loves the other for the sake of itself; spiritual love loves the other for the sake of Christ. That is why self-centered love seeks direct contact with other persons. It loves them, not as free persons, but as those whom it binds to itself. It wants to do everything it can to win and conquer; it puts pressure on the other person. It desires to be irresistible, to dominate. Self-centered love does not think much of truth. It makes the truth relative, since nothing, not even the truth, must come between it and the person loved. Emotional, self-centered love desires other persons, their company. It wants them to return its love, but it does not serve them. On the contrary, it continues to desire even when it seems to be serving.

—from *Life Together* 42

Emotional Community

Two factors, which are really one and the same thing, reveal the difference between spiritual and self-centered love. Emotional, self-centered love cannot tolerate the dissolution of a community that has become false, even for the sake of genuine community. And such self-centered love cannot love an enemy, that is to say, one who seriously and stubbornly resists it. Both spring from the same source: emotional love is by its very nature desire, desire for self-centered community. As long as it can possibly satisfy this desire, it will not give it up, even for the sake of truth, even for the sake of genuine love for others. But emotional, self-centered love is at an end when it can no longer expect its desire to be fulfilled, namely, in the face of an enemy. There it turns into hatred, contempt, and slander.

—from *Life Together* 43

Christ Between

Christ stands between me and others. I do not know in advance what love of others means on the basis of the general idea of love that grows out of my emotional desires. All this may instead be hatred and the worst kind of selfishness in the yes of Christ. Only Christ in his Word tells me what love is. Contrary to all my own opinions and convictions, Jesus Christ will tell me what love for my brothers and sisters really looks like. Therefore, spiritual love is bound to the word of Jesus Christ alone. Where Christ tells me to maintain community for the sake of love, I desire to maintain it. Where the truth of Christ orders me to dissolve a community for the sake of love, I will dissolve it, despite all the protests of my self-centered love. Because spiritual love does not desire but rather serves, it loves an enemy as a brother or sister. It originates neither in the brother or sister nor in the enemy, but in Christ and his word. Self-centered, emotional love can never comprehend spiritual love, for spiritual love is from above. It is something completely strange, new, and incomprehensible to all earthly love.

—from *Life Together* 43

Unmediated Community

Because Christ stands between me and another, I must not long for unmediated community with that person. As only Christ was able to speak to me in such a way that I was helped, so others too can only be helped by Christ alone. However, this means that I must release others from all my attempts to control, coerce, and dominate them with my love. In their freedom from me, other persons want to be loved for who they are, as those for whom Christ became a human being, died, and rose again, as those for whom Christ won the forgiveness of sins and prepared eternal life. Because Christ has long since acted decisively for other Christians, before I could begin to act, I must allow them the freedom to be Christ's. They should encounter me only as the persons they already are in Christ. This is the meaning of the claim that we can encounter others only through the mediation of Christ. Self-centered love constructs its own image of other persons, about what they are and what they should become. It takes the life of the other person into its own hands. Spiritual love recognizes the true image of the other person as seen from the perspective of Jesus Christ. It is the image Jesus Christ has formed and wants to form in all people.

—from *Life Together* 43–44

On November 15, 1931, Bonhoeffer is ordained.

Spiritual Love

Spiritual love will prove successful insofar as it commends Christ to the other in all that it says and does. It will not seek to agitate another by exerting all too personal, direct influence or by crudely interfering in one's life. It will not take pleasure in pious, emotional fervor and excitement. Rather, it will encounter the other with the clear word of God and be prepared to leave the other alone with this word for a long time. It will be willing to release others again so that Christ may deal with them. It will respect the other as the boundary that Christ establishes between us; and it will find full community with the other in the Christ who alone binds us together. This spiritual love will thus speak to Christ about the other Christian more than to the other Christian about Christ. It knows that the most direct way to others is always through prayer to Christ and that love of the other is completely tied to the truth found in Christ. It is out of this love that John the disciple speaks: "I have no greater joy than this, to hear that my children are walking in the truth" (3 John 4).

—from *Life Together* 44

The Community as Church

The existence of any Christian communal life essentially depends on whether or not it succeeds at the right time in promoting the ability to distinguish between a human ideal and God's reality, between spiritual and emotional community. The life and death of a Christian community is decided by its ability to reach sober clarity on these points as soon as possible. In other words, a life together under the Word will stay healthy only when it does not form itself into a movement, an order, a society, a *collegium pietatis*, but instead understands itself as being part of the one, holy, universal, Christian church, sharing through its deeds and suffering in the hardships and struggles and promise of the whole church. Every principle of selection, and every division connected with it that is not necessitated quite objectively by common work, local conditions, or family connections is of the greatest danger to a Christian community. Self-centeredness always insinuates itself in any process of intellectual or spiritual selectivity, destroying the spiritual power of the community and robbing the community of its effectiveness for the church, thus driving it into sectarianism. The exclusion of the weak and insignificant, the seemingly useless people, from everyday Christian life in community may actually mean the exclusion of Christ; for in the poor sister or brother, Christ is knocking at the door. We must, therefore, be very careful on this point.

—from *Life Together* 45–46

Real Community

Whenever a community of a purely spiritual nature comes together, the danger is uncannily near that everything pertaining to self-centeredness will be brought into and intermixed with this community. Purely spiritual life in community is not only dangerous but also not normal. Whenever physical-familial community, the community formed among those engaged in serious work or everyday life with all its demands on working people, is not introduced into the spiritual community, extraordinary vigilance and clear thinking are called for. That is why it is precisely on short retreats that, as experience has shown, self-centeredness develops most easily. Nothing is easier than to stimulate the euphoria of community in a few days of life together; and nothing is more fatal to the healthy, sober, everyday life in community of Christians.

—from *Life Together* 46–47

This Is Us

The human being, accepted, judged, and awakened to new life by God—this is Jesus Christ, this is the whole of humanity in Christ, this is us. The form of Jesus Christ alone victoriously encounters the world. From this form proceeds all the formation of a world reconciled with God. The word "formation" arouses our suspicion. We are tired of Christian agendas. We are tired of the thoughtless, superficial slogan of a so-called practical Christianity to replace a so-called dogmatic Christianity. We have seen that the forces which form the world come from entirely other sources than Christianity, and that so-called practical Christianity has failed in the world just as much as so-called dogmatic Christianity. Hence we must understand by "formation" something quite different from what we are accustomed to mean, and in fact the Holy Scripture speaks of formation in a sense that at first sounds quite strange. It is not primarily concerned with formation of the world by planning and programs, but in all formation it is concerned only with the one form that has overcome the world, the form of Jesus Christ. . . . Formation occurs only by being drawn into the form of Jesus Christ, by *being conformed to the unique form of the one who became human, was crucified, and is risen.* This does not happen as we strive "to become like Jesus," as we customarily say, but as the form of Jesus Christ himself so works on us that it molds us, conforming our form to Christ's own (Gal. 4:9).

—from *Ethics* 92–93

Formed by Christ

Christ remains the only one who forms. Christian people do not form the world with their ideas. Rather, Christ forms human beings to a form the same as Christ's own. However, just as the form of Christ is misperceived where he is understood essentially as the teacher of a pious and good life, so formation of human beings is also wrongly understood where one sees it only as guidance for a pious and good life. Christ is the one who has become human, who was crucified, and who is risen, as confessed by the Christian faith. . . . To be conformed to the one who has become human—that is what being really human means. . . . All super-humanity, all efforts to outgrow one's nature as human, all struggle to be heroic or a demigod, all fall away from a person here, because they are untrue. The real human being is the object neither of contempt nor of deification, but the object of the love of God. . . . To be conformed with the one who became human means that we may be the human beings that we really are. Pretension, hypocrisy, compulsion, forcing oneself to be something different, better, more ideal than one is—all are abolished. God loves the real human being. God became a real human being.

—from *Ethics* 93–94

Humanity and Christ

In Christ the form of humanity was created anew. What was at stake was not a matter of place, time, climate, race, individual, society, religion, or taste, but nothing less than the life of humanity, which recognized here its image and its hope. What happened to Christ happened to humanity. There is no explaining the mystery that only a part of humanity recognizes the form of its savior. The desire of the one who has become human to take form in all human beings remains to this hour unsatisfied. He who bore the form of *the* human being can only take form in a small flock; this is Christ's church.

—from *Ethics* 96

The Body and the Church

The New Testament, in deep and clear indication of the matter itself, calls the church the body of Christ. The body is the form. So the church is not a religious community of those who revere Christ, but Christ who has taken form among human beings. The church may be called the body of Christ because in the body of Jesus Christ *human being per se,* and therefore all human beings, have really been taken on. The church now bears the form that in truth is meant for all people. The image according to which it is being formed is the image of humanity. What takes place in the church happens vicariously and representatively as a model for all human beings. But it cannot be said too clearly that not even the church is a self-determined form apart from the form of Jesus Christ; therefore it can never claim rights, authority, and dignity independently and on its own, apart from Jesus Christ. The church is nothing but that piece of humanity where Christ really has taken form. . . . Therefore essentially its first concern is not with the so-called religious functions of human beings, but with the existence in the world of whole human beings in all their relationships. The church's concern is not religion, but the form of Christ and its taking form among a band of people.

—from *Ethics* 96–97

Humanity's True Form

We have recognized that we can speak of formation in a Christian-ethical reflection only by focusing on the form of Jesus Christ. Formation is not an independent process or condition that can somehow be detached from this form. Formation happens only from and toward this form of Jesus Christ. The starting point of Christian ethics is the body of Christ, the form of Christ in the form of the church, the formation of the church according to the form of Christ. Only to the extent that what happens to the church truly concerns all humanity is the concept of formation—indirectly—meaningful for all human beings. But here again it is not as if the church has been set out as a model for the world, so to speak. Rather, we can only speak of the formation of the world in such a way that we address humanity in the light of its true form, which belongs to it, which it has already received, but which it has not grasped and accepted, namely, the form of Jesus Christ that is its own. Thus humanity is—so to speak, proleptically—drawn into the church. It is still the case that, even where one talks about the formation of the world, only the form of Jesus Christ is meant.

—from *Ethics* 97–98

Real Humanity

Christ is not a principle according to which the whole world must be formed. Christ does not proclaim a system of that which would be good today, here, and at all times. Christ does not teach an abstract ethic that must be carried out, cost what it may. Christ was not essentially a teacher, a lawgiver, but a human being, a real human being like us. Accordingly, Christ does not want us to be first of all pupils, representatives, and advocates of a particular doctrine, but human beings, real human beings before God. Christ did not, like an ethicist, love a theory about the good; he loved real people. Christ was not interested, like a philosopher, in what is "generally valid," but in that which serves real concrete human beings. Christ was not concerned about whether "the maxim of an action" could become "a principle of universal law," but whether my action now helps *my* neighbor to be a human being before God. God did not become an idea, a principle, a program, a universally valid belief, or a law; God became human. . . . Formation according to the form of Christ includes, therefore, two things: that the form of Christ remains one and the same, not as a general idea but as the one who Christ uniquely is, the God who became human, was crucified, and is risen; and that precisely because of the form of Christ the form of the real human being is preserved, so that the *real human being receives the form of Christ.*

—from *Ethics* 98–99

Unfruitful Abstraction

The issue is the process by which Christ takes form among us. Therefore the issue is the real, judged, and renewed human being. The real, the judged, and the renewed human being exists only in the form of Jesus Christ and therefore in being conformed to Christ. Only the person taken on in Christ is the real human being; only the person confronted by the cross of Christ is the judged human being; only the person who participates in the resurrection of Christ is the renewed human being. Since God became a human being in Christ, all thinking about human beings without Christ is unfruitful abstraction. The counter-image to the human being taken up into the form of Christ is the human being as self-creator, self-judge, and self-renewer; these people bypass their true humanity and therefore, sooner or later, destroy themselves. Falling away from Christ is at the same time falling away from one's own true nature.

—from *Ethics* 134

Turning Back

There is only one way to turn back, and that is acknowledgment of guilt toward Christ. The guilt we must acknowledge is not the occasional mistake or going astray, not the breaking of an abstract law, but falling away from Christ, from the form of the One who would take form in us and lead us to our own true form. Genuine acknowledgment of guilt does not grow from experiences of dissolution and decay but, for us who have encountered Christ, only by looking at the form Christ has taken. It presupposes, therefore, some degree of community with this form. Therein lies the miracle. How can those who have fallen away from Christ still have community with Christ, except by the grace with which Christ holds fast the fallen and preserves that community with them? Acknowledgment of guilt is based only on the grace of Christ, because of Christ's reaching out for those who have fallen. With this acknowledgment, the process of human conformation with Christ begins. Thus, this acknowledgment of guilt is distinguished from all other self-generated and unfruitful acknowledgments.

—from *Ethics* 135

The Church of Christ

The place where this acknowledgment of guilt becomes real is the church. This does not mean that the church, alongside other things it is and does, is also the place where guilt is genuinely acknowledged. Instead, the church is that community of people that has been led by the grace of Christ to acknowledge its guilt toward Christ. It is tautological to say that the church is the place where guilt is acknowledged. If it were otherwise, the church would no longer be church. The church is today the community of people who, grasped by the power of Christ's grace, acknowledge, confess, and take upon themselves not only their personal sins, but also the Western world's falling away from Jesus Christ as guilt toward Jesus Christ. The church is where Jesus makes his form real in the midst of the world. Therefore only the church can be the place of personal and corporate rebirth and renewal.

—from *Ethics* 135

Life in Prison

Of course people outside find it difficult to imagine what prison life is like. The situation in itself—that is each single moment—is perhaps not so very different here from anywhere else; I read, meditate, write, pace up and down my cell—without rubbing myself sore against the walls like a polar bear. The great thing is to stick to what one still has and can do—there is still plenty left—and not to be dominated by the thought of what one cannot do, and by feelings of resentment and discontent. I am sure I never realized as clearly as I do here what the Bible and Luther mean by "temptation." Quite suddenly, and for no apparent physical or psychological reason, the peace and composure that were supporting one are jarred, and the heart becomes, in Jeremiah's expressive phrase, "deceitful above all things, and desperately corrupt; who can understand it?" It feels like an invasion from outside, as if by evil powers trying to rob one of what is most vital. But no doubt these experiences are good and necessary, as they teach one to understand human life better.

—from *Letters and Papers from Prison* 22–23

Stripped Bare

In spite of everything that I have so far written, things here are revolting, . . . my grim experiences often pursue me into the night and . . . I can shake them off only by reciting one hymn after another, and that I am apt to wake up with a sigh rather than with a hymn of praise to God. It is possible to get used to physical hardships, and to live for months out of the body, so to speak—almost too much so—but one does not get used to the psychological strain; on the contrary, I have the feeling that everything that I see and hear is putting years on me and that I am often finding the world nauseating and burdensome. . . . I often wonder who I really am—the man who goes on squirming under these ghastly experiences in wretchedness that cries to heaven, or the man who scourges himself and pretends to others (and even to himself) that he is placid, cheerful, composed, and in control of himself, and allows people to admire him for it (i.e., for playing the part—or is it not playing a part?). What does one's attitude mean, anyway? In short, I know less than ever about myself, and I am no longer attaching any importance to it. I have had more than enough psychology, and I am less and less inclined to analyze the state of my soul. . . . There is something more at stake than self-knowledge.

—from *Letters and Papers from Prison* 89–90

Hope for Today

I can (I hope) bear all things "in faith," even my condemnation, and even the other consequences that I fear (Ps. 18:29); but to be anxiously looking ahead wears one down. Don't worry about me if something worse happens. Other brothers and sisters have already been through that. But faithless vacillation, endless deliberation without action, refusal to take any risks—that is a real danger. I must be able to know for certain that I am in God's hands, not in those of people. Then everything becomes easy, even the severest privation. It is not now a matter (I think I can say this truthfully) of my being "understandably impatient," as people are probably saying, but of my facing everything in faith.

—from *Letters and Papers from Prison* 99

December

The Reality of Jesus

The divine mandate of the church is the commission of allowing the reality of Jesus Christ to become real in proclamation, church order, and Christian life—in short, its concern is the eternal salvation of the whole world. The mandate of the church embraces all people as they live within all the other mandates. Since a person is at the same time worker, spouse, and citizen, since one mandate overlaps with the others, and since all the mandates need to be fulfilled at the same time, so the church mandate reaches into all the other mandates. Similarly, the Christian is at the same time worker, spouse, and citizen. Every division into separate realms is forbidden here. Human beings as whole persons stand before the whole earthly and eternal reality that God in Jesus Christ has prepared for them. Only in full response to the whole of this offer and this claim can the human person fulfill this reality. This is the witness the church has to give to the world, that all the other mandates are not there to divide people and tear them apart but to deal with them as whole people before God the Creator, Reconciler, and Redeemer—that reality in all its manifold aspects is ultimately *one* in God who became human, Jesus Christ.

—from *Ethics* 73

The Consequence of Faith

We think we understand when we hear that obedience is possible only where there is faith. Does not obedience follow faith as good fruit grows on a good tree? First, faith, then obedience. If by that we mean that it is faith which justifies, and not the act of obedience, all well and good, for that is the essential and unexceptional presupposition of all that follows. If, however, we make a chronological distinction between faith and obedience, and make obedience subsequent to faith, we are divorcing the one from the other—and then we get the practical question, when must obedience begin? Obedience remains separated from faith. From the point of view of justification it is necessary thus to separate them, but we must never lost sight of their essential unity. For faith is only real when there is obedience, never without it, and faith only becomes faith in the act of obedience. Since, then, we cannot adequately speak of obedience as the consequence of faith, and since we must never forget the indissoluble unity of the two, we must place the one proposition that only those who believe are obedient alongside the other, that only those who are obedient believe. In the one case faith is the condition of obedience, and in the other obedience the condition of faith. In exactly the same way in which obedience is called the consequence of faith, it must also be called the presupposition of faith.

—from *A Testament to Freedom* 310–311

Space for God

I've come to be doubtful of talking about any human boundaries (is even death, which people now hardly fear, and is sin, which they now hardly understand, still a genuine boundary today?). It always seems to me that we are trying anxiously in this way to reserve some space for God; I should like to speak of God not on the boundaries but at the center, not in weakness but in strength; and therefore not in death and guilt but in humanity's life and goodness. As to the boundaries, it seems to me better to be silent and leave the insoluble unsolved. Belief in the resurrection is *not* the "solution" of the problem of death. God's "beyond" is not the beyond of our cognitive faculties. The transcendence of epistemological theory has nothing to do with the transcendence of God. God is beyond in the midst of our life. The church stands, not at the boundaries where human powers give out, but in the middle of the village. That is how it is in the Old Testament, and in this sense we still read the New Testament far too little in the light of the Old.

—from *A Testament to Freedom* 503

The Blessing

You think the Bible has not much to say about health, fortune, vigor, etc. I have been thinking over that again. It is certainly not true of the Old Testament. The intermediate theological category between God and human fortune is, as far as I can see, that of blessing. In the Old Testament—e.g., among the patriarchs—there is a concern, not for fortune, but for God's blessing, which includes in itself all earthly good. In that blessing the whole of earthly life is claimed for God, and it includes all God's promises. It would be natural to suppose that, as usual, the New Testament spiritualizes the teaching of the Old Testament here, and therefore to regard the Old Testament blessing as superseded in the New. But is it an accident that sickness and death are mentioned in connection with the misuse of the Lord's Supper ("The cup of *blessing*" 1 Cor. 10:16; 11:30), that Jesus restored people's health, and that while his disciples were with him they "lacked nothing"?

—from *Letters and Papers from Prison* 197

The Blessed

Now, is it right to set the Old Testament blessing against the cross? That is what Kierkegaard did. That makes the cross, or at least suffering, an abstract principle; and that is just what gives rise to an unhealthy methodism, which deprives suffering of its element of contingency on a divine ordinance. It is true that in the Old Testament the person who receives the blessing has to endure a great deal of suffering (e.g., Abraham, Isaac, Jacob, and Joseph), but this never leads to the idea that fortune and suffering, blessing and cross are mutually exclusive and contradictory—nor does it in the New Testament. Indeed, the only difference between the Old and New Testaments in this respect is that in the Old the blessing includes the cross, and in the New the cross includes the blessing.

—from *Letters and Papers from Prison* 197–198

The Need for Joy

Since ancient times, *acidia*—sorrowfulness of the heart, "resignation"—has been one of the deadly sins. "Serve the Lord with gladness" (Ps. 100:2) summons us to the Scriptures. This is what our life has been given to us for, what it has been preserved for up till now. Joy belongs, not only to those who have been called home, but also to the living, and no one shall take it from us. We are one with them in this joy, but never in sorrow. . . . Joy dwells with God; it descends from God and seizes spirit, soul, and body, and where this joy has grasped us it grows greater, carries us away, opens closed doors. There is a joy which knows nothing of sorrow, need, and anxiety of the heart; it has no duration, and it can only drug one for the moment. The joy of God has been through the poverty of the crib and the distress of the cross; therefore it is insuperable, irrefutable. It does not deny the distress where it is, but finds God in the midst of it, indeed precisely there; it does not contest the most grievous sin, but finds forgiveness in just this way; it looks death in the face, yet finds life in death itself. We are concerned with this joy which has overcome. It alone is worth believing; it alone helps and heals.

—from *A Testament to Freedom* 458

God's Instruments

Christ kept himself from suffering till his hour had come, but when it did come he met it as a free man, seized it, and mastered it. Christ, so the Scriptures tell us, bore the sufferings of all humanity in his own body as if they were his own—a thought beyond our comprehension—accepting them of his own free will. We are certainly not Christ; we are not called on to redeem the world by our own deeds and sufferings, and we need not try to assume such an impossible burden. We are not lords, but instruments in the hand of the Lord of history; and we can share in other people's sufferings only in a very limited degree. We are not Christ, but if we want to be Christians, we must have some share in Christ's large-heartedness by acting with responsibility and in freedom when the hour of danger comes, and by showing a real sympathy that springs, not from fear, but from the liberating and redeeming love of Christ for all who suffer. Mere waiting and looking on is not Christian behavior. Christians are called to sympathy and action, not in the first place by our personal sufferings, but by the sufferings of our brothers and sisters, for whose sake Christ suffered.

—from *Letters and Papers from Prison* 14

Living with Yearning

I myself have lived for many, many years quite absorbed in aims and tasks and hopes without any personal hankerings; and perhaps that has made me old before my time. It has made everything too "matter-of-fact." Almost everyone has aims and tasks, and everything is objectified, reified to such a tremendous extent—how many people today allow themselves any strong personal feeling and real yearning, or take the trouble to spend their strength freely in working out and carrying out that yearning, and letting it bear fruit? Those sentimental radio hits, with their artificial naïveté and empty crudities, are the pitiful remains and the maximum that people will tolerate by way of mental effort; it is a ghastly desolation and impoverishment. By contrast, we can be very glad when something affects us deeply and regard the accompanying pains as an enrichment. High tensions produce big sparks (is that not a physical fact? If it is not, then translate it into the right kind of language).

—from *Letters and Papers from Prison* 134–135

A Share in Suffering

It is only by living completely in this world that one learns to have faith. One must completely abandon any attempt to make something of oneself, whether it be a saint, or a converted sinner, or a chuchman (a so-called priestly type!), a righteous person or an unrighteous one, a sick person or a healthy one. By this-worldliness I mean living unreservedly in life's duties, problems, successes and failures, experiences and perplexities. In so doing we throw ourselves completely into the arms of God, taking seriously, not our own sufferings, but those of God in the world—watching with Christ in Gethsemane. That, I think, is faith; that is *metanoia*; and that is how one becomes human and a Christian. How can success make us arrogant, or failure lead us astray, when we share in God's sufferings through a life of this kind?

—from *A Testament to Freedom* 510

Reality in Christ

In Jesus Christ the reality of God has entered into the reality of this world. The place where the questions about the reality of God and about the reality of the world are answered at the same time is characterized solely by the name: Jesus Christ. God and the world are enclosed in this name. In Christ all things exist (Col. 1:17). From now on we cannot speak rightly of either God or the world without speaking of Jesus Christ. All concepts of reality that ignore Jesus Christ are abstractions. All thinking about the good that plays off what ought to be against what is, or what is against what ought to be, is overcome where the good has become reality, namely, in Jesus Christ. Jesus Christ cannot be identified either with an ideal, a norm, or with what exists. The enmity of the ideal toward what exists, the fanatical imposition of an idea on an existing entity that resists it, can be as far from the good as the surrender of the ought to the expedient. The ought as well as the expedient receive in Christ a completely new meaning. The irreconcilable opposition of ought to be and is finds reconciliation in Christ, that is, in ultimate reality. To participate in this reality is the true meaning of the question concerning the good.

—from *Ethics* 54–55

God and the World

In Christ we are invited to participate in the reality of God and the reality of the world at the same time, the one not without the other. The reality of God is disclosed only as it places me completely into the reality of the world. But I find the reality of the world, always already borne, accepted, and reconciled in the reality of God. That is the mystery of the revelation of God in the human being Jesus Christ. The Christian ethic asks, then, how this reality of God and of the world that is given in Christ becomes real in our world. It is not as if "our world" were something outside this God-world reality that is in Christ, as if it did not already belong to the world borne, accepted, and reconciled in Christ; it is not, therefore, as if some "principle" must first be applied to our circumstances and our time. Rather the question is how the reality in Christ—which has long embraced us and our world within itself—works here and now or, in other words, how life is to be lived in it. What matters is *participating in the reality of God and the world in Jesus Christ today*, and doing so in such a way that I never experience the reality of God without the reality of the world, nor the reality of the world without the reality of God.

—from *Ethics* 55

Christ's Call

The preaching and sacrament of the church is the place where Jesus Christ is present. To hear Jesus's call to discipleship, one needs no personal revelation. Listen to the preaching and receive the sacrament! Listen to the gospel of the crucified and risen Lord! Here he is, the whole Christ, the very same who encountered the disciples. Indeed, here he is already present as the glorified, the victorious, the living Christ. No one but Christ himself can call us to discipleship. Discipleship in essence never consists in a decision for this or that specific action; it is always a decision for or against Jesus Christ. And this is exactly why the situation was not any less ambiguous for the disciple or the tax collector who was called by him than it is for us today. The obedience of those who were first called constituted discipleship precisely in that they recognized Christ in the one who was calling them. For them, as for us, it is the hidden Christ who calls. The call as such is ambiguous. What counts is not the call as such, but the one who calls. But Christ can only be recognized in faith. That was true in the same way for the first disciples as it is for us. They saw the rabbi and the miracle worker, and believed in Christ. We hear the word and believe in Christ.

—from *Discipleship* 202

Recognizing Christ

But did those first disciples not have an advantage over us in that, once they had recognized Christ, they received his unambiguous command from his very own lips and were told what to do? And are we not left to our own devices precisely at this crucial point of Christian obedience? Does not the same Christ speak differently to us than he spoke to them? If this were true, then we would indeed be in a hopeless situation. But it is far from true. Christ speaks to us exactly as he spoke to them. For the first disciples of Jesus it was also not as if they first recognized him as the Christ, and then received his command. Rather, it was only through his word and his command that they recognized him. They trusted in his word and his command, and thereby recognized Him as the Christ.

—from *Discipleship* 202

The Word of Christ

There was no other way for the disciples to know Christ than through his clear word. Conversely, therefore, to recognize Jesus truly as the Christ necessarily included a recognition of his will. To recognize the person of Jesus Christ did not undermine the disciples' certainty about what to do, but on the contrary created that certainty. Indeed, there is no other way to recognize Christ. If Christ is the living Lord of my life, then I am addressed by his word whenever I encounter him; indeed, I do not really know him except through his clear word and command. There are those who object that this is precisely our dilemma: we would like to know Christ and have faith in him, and yet we are unable to recognize his will. This objection, however, springs from a vague and mistaken knowledge of Christ. To know Christ means to recognize him in his word as Lord and savior of my life.

—from *Discipleship* 203

Then and Now

All this makes it abundantly clear that we cannot play off the narrative of the calling of the disciples against other parts of the gospel account. It is never a question of our having or taking on the same identity as the disciples or other people in the New Testament. The only issue of importance is that Jesus Christ and his call are the same, then and now. His word remains one and the same, whether it was spoken during his earthly life or today, whether it was addressed to the disciples or to the paralytic. Then and now, it is the gracious call to enter his kingdom and to submit to his rule. The question whether I ought to compare myself with the disciple or with the paralytic poses a dangerous and false alternative. I need not compare myself with either of them. Instead, all I have to do is to listen and do Christ's word and will as I receive them in both of these biblical accounts. Scripture does not present us with a collection of Christian types to be imitated according to our own choice. Rather, in every passage it proclaims to us the one Jesus Christ. It is him alone whom I ought to hear. He is one and the same everywhere.

—from *Discipleship* 203–204

A Shiver of Fear

When the old Christianity spoke of the return of the Lord Jesus, they thought of a great day of judgment. Even though this thought may appear to us to be so unlike Christmas, it is original Christianity and to be taken extremely seriously. When we hear Jesus knocking, our conscience first of all pricks us: Are we rightly prepared? Is our heart capable of becoming God's dwelling place? Thus Advent becomes a time of self-examination. . . . It is very remarkable that we face the thought that God is coming so calmly, whereas previously peoples trembled at the day of God, whereas the world fell into trembling when Jesus Christ walked over the earth. That is why it is so strange when we see the marks of God in the world so often together with the marks of human suffering, with the marks of the cross on Golgotha. We have become so accustomed to the idea of divine love and of God's coming at Christmas that we no longer feel the shiver of fear that God's coming should arouse in us. We are indifferent to the message, taking only the pleasant and agreeable out of it and forgetting the serious aspect, that the God of the world draws near to the people of our little earth and lays claim to us. The coming of God is truly not only glad tidings, but first of all frightening news for every one who has a conscience.

—from *A Testament to Freedom* 185

The Terror of Christmas

Only when we have felt the terror of the matter [of God's coming at Christmas], can we recognize the incomparable kindness. God comes into the very midst of evil and of death, and judges the evil in us and in the world. And by judging us, God cleanses and sanctifies us, comes to us with grace and love. God makes us happy as only children can be happy. God wants to always be with us, wherever we may be—in our sin, in our suffering and death. We are no longer alone; God is with us. We are no longer homeless; a bit of the eternal home itself has moved into us. Therefore we adults can rejoice deeply within our hearts under the Christmas tree, perhaps much more than the children are able. We know that God's goodness will once again draw near. We think of all of God's goodness that came our way last year and sense something of this marvelous home. Jesus comes in judgment and grace: "Behold I stand at the door . . . Open wide the gates!" (Ps. 24:7)

—from *A Testament to Freedom* 185–186

Christ Our Neighbor

One day, at the last judgment, he will separate the sheep and the goats and will say to those on his right: "Come, you blessed, . . . I was hungry and you fed me. . . ." (Matt. 25:34ff). To the astonished question of when and where, he answered: "What you did to the least of these, you have done to me. . . ." (Matt. 25:40). With that we are faced with the shocking reality: Jesus stands at the door and knocks, in complete reality. He asks you for help in the form of a beggar, in the form of a ruined human being in torn clothing. He confronts you in every person that you meet. Christ walks on the earth as your neighbor as long as there are people. He walks on the earth as the one through whom God calls you, speaks to you, and makes his demands. That is the greatest seriousness and the greatest blessedness of the Advent message. Christ stands at the door. He lives in the form of the person in our midst. Will you keep the door locked or open it to him?

—from *A Testament to Freedom* 186

Advent for the Thirsty

"Now when these things begin to take place, look up and raise your heads, because your redemption is drawing near" (Luke 21:28). This word is not addressed to all those who have become so accustomed to their condition that they no longer notice they are captives; people who have put up with their plight for all kinds of reasons and have become so apathetic that they are not provoked when someone calls out to them, "Your redemption is near." This Advent word is not meant for the well fed and satisfied, but for those who hunger and thirst. There is a knocking at their door, powerful and insistent. And like [a] miner buried alive in the mine, we hear every blow, every step closer the rescuer takes with extreme alertness. Can one even imagine that the miner ever thought of anything other than the approaching liberation from the moment he heard the first tapping against the rock? And now the first Sunday in Advent tells us nothing else: "Your redemption is drawing near!" It is already knocking at the door, don't you hear it? It is breaking open its way through the rubble and hard rock of your life and heart.

—from *A Testament to Freedom* 224

The Advent Rescue

Christ is breaking open his way to you. He wants to again soften your heart, which has become hard. In these weeks of Advent while we are waiting for Christmas, he calls to us that he is coming and that he will rescue us from the prison of our existence, from fear, guilt, and loneliness. . . . Let us make no mistake about it. Redemption is drawing near. Only the question is: Will we let it come to us as well or will we resist it? Will we let ourselves be pulled into this movement coming down from heaven to earth or will we refuse to have anything to do with it? Either with us or without us, Christmas will come. It is up to each individual to decide what it will be.

—from *A Testament to Freedom* 224–225

Look Up!

Look up, you whose eyes are fixed on this earth, you who are captivated by the events and changes on the surface of this earth. Look up, you who turned away from heaven to this ground because you had become disillusioned. Look up, you whose eyes are laden with tears, you who mourn the loss of all that the earth has snatched away. Look up, you who cannot lift your eyes because you are so laden with guilt. "Look up, your redemption is drawing near." Something different than you see daily, something more important, something infinitely greater and more powerful is taking place. Become aware of it, be on guard, wait a short while longer, wait and something new will overtake you! God will come, Jesus will take possession of you and you will be redeemed people! Lift up your heads, you army of the afflicted, the humbled, the discouraged, you defeated army with bowed heads. The battle is not lost, the victory is yours—take courage, be strong! There is no room here for shaking your heads and doubting, because Christ is coming.

—from *A Testament to Freedom* 225

The Comfort of Tradition

It is not till such times as these that we realize what it means to possess a past and a spiritual inheritance independent of changes of time and circumstance. The consciousness of being borne up by a spiritual tradition that goes back for centuries gives one a feeling of confidence and security in the face of all passing strains and stresses. I believe that anyone who is aware of such reserves of strength need not be ashamed of more tender feelings evoked by the memory of a rich and noble past, for in my opinion they belong to the better and nobler part of mankind. They will not overwhelm those who hold fast to values that no one can take from them.

—from *Letters and Papers from Prison* 57

Christmas in Prison

From the Christian point of view there is no special problem about Christmas in a prison cell. For many people in this building it will probably be a more sincere and genuine occasion than in places where nothing but the name is kept. That misery, suffering, poverty, loneliness, helplessness, and guilt mean something quite different in the eyes of God from what they mean in the judgment of humans, that God will approach where men and women turn away, that Christ was born in a stable because there was no room for him in the inn—these are things that a prisoner can understand better than other people; for him they really are glad tidings, and that faith gives him a part in the communion of saints, a Christian fellowship breaking the bounds of time and space and reducing the months of confinement here to insignificance.

—from *Letters and Papers from Prison* 57

The Birth of Theology

No priest, no theologian stood at the cradle in Bethlehem. And yet all Christian theology has its origin in the wonder of all wonders, that God became human. . . . *Theologia sacra* arises from those on bended knees who do homage to the mystery of the divine child in the stall. Israel had no theology. It did not know God in the flesh. Without the holy night there is no theology. "God revealed in the flesh," the God-human Jesus Christ, is the holy mystery which theology is appointed to guard. What a mistake to think that it is the task of theology to unravel God's mystery, to bring it down to the flat, ordinary human wisdom of experience and reason! It is the task of theology solely to preserve God's wonder as wonder, to understand, to defend, to glorify God's mystery as mystery. . . . Surely Christmas Eve can kindle in us again something like a love of sacred theology, so that, seized and compelled by the wonder of the cradle of the Son of God, we are moved to consider again, reverently, the mysteries of God.

—from *A Testament to Freedom* 448

God's Human Nature

The Fathers were concerned to say that God, the Son, assumed *human nature*, not that God assumed *a man*. What does that mean? God became human by assuming human nature, not by taking an individual man. This distinction was necessary to preserve the universality of the wonder of Christmas. "Human nature," that is, the nature, essence, flesh of all people, i.e., my nature, my flesh; human nature, that is, the embodiment of all human possibilities. Perhaps we moderns might put it more simply by saying that in the birth of Jesus Christ, God took on human nature, and not just an individual man. But this taking happened corporeally, and that is the unique wonder of the incarnation. . . . Because Christmas is the physical acceptance of all human flesh by the gracious God, we must affirm that God's Son took human nature upon himself.

—from *A Testament to Freedom* 449

Our Flesh

The body of Jesus Christ is our flesh. He bears our flesh. Therefore, where Jesus Christ is, there we are, whether we know it or
not; that is true because of the Incarnation. What happens to Jesus
Christ, happens to us. It really is all *our* "poor flesh and blood"
which lies there in the crib; it is *our* flesh which dies with him on
the cross and is buried with him. He took human nature so that
we might be eternally with him. Where the body of Jesus Christ
is, there are we; indeed, we are his body. So the Christmas message
for all people runs: You are accepted, God has not despised you,
but he bears in his body all your flesh and blood. Look at the
cradle! In the body of the little child, in the incarnate Son of God,
your flesh, all your distress, anxiety, temptation, indeed all your sin,
is borne, forgiven, and healed.

—from *A Testament to Freedom* 449

God's Merciful Action

In the feast of Christmas we are directed in a new way to the very thing that stands in the center of the Bible, to the simple reality of the gracious and merciful action which comes from God into this lost world. We are no longer concerned with elegant and gay pictures and fancies; from the reality which is so plain and from our distress, we thirst for the reality of the great divine help. Our question is whether God really has sent the One who has the right and authority for complete, all-embracing, final redemption. And the Christmas message is the complete, glorious "Yes" of the answer to this question.

—from *A Testament to Freedom* 453

The Simple Message

It is our task, our blessed task, at Christmas to hear the message in all its simplicity and to utter it just as it stands. The world has always been full of thousands of demands, plans, summonses, exhortations with which people seek to overcome the distress of the world, which sooner or later, sadly enough, becomes evident to everyone. We do not have to demand, to plan, and to exhort again, thank God, we simply have to hear and to say what has been given by God as our real, our complete hope, without any of our doing and our working. . . . We simply have the Christmas which the shepherds of Bethlehem had, even if we can take the whole richness of the cross, the resurrection, and the ascension of Christ into our Christmas.

—from *A Testament to Freedom* 453–454

Listen and Believe

Like the shepherds, we remain believers. Like them, we see the child in the cradle, who does not want to be distinguished from other children, and we hear the message "as it has been told them" of this child. The night of the world is as dark to us as it was to the shepherds then. We can no more see now than they could then that the glory of the world is laid on the shoulders of this child, that all power in heaven and earth is given to him, despite all the rich and blessed experiences of all Christendom on earth; today, we can do no more than listen and believe as they did then.

—from *A Testament to Freedom* 454

God's Hand on the World

Our Christmas, too, does not take us out of the distress, the burdens of our life in the world; it does not take us to paradise. We too must return again, like the shepherds, back into the old conditions, with all the pressure that chafes us. But—only let the shepherds' Christmas be given us if like them we can just hear and believe! The Savior is there! God's hand again rests upon the world and will no longer let it go! The night is far spent, the day is already at hand! The glory of the world has already been taken from the prince of this world and laid on the shoulders of this child! In that case it can also be said of us, as of those shepherds: not only did they "return" into all the old, bitter distress; they also "glorified and praised God for all they had heard and seen, as it had been told them," in the midst of all their personal needs, in the midst of the night of the world, in the midst of war.

—from *A Testament to Freedom* 454

A Life Well Lived

I am so sure of God's guiding hand that I hope I shall always be kept in that certainty. You must never doubt that I am traveling with gratitude and cheerfulness along the road where I am being led. My past life is brim-full of God's goodness, and my sins are covered by the forgiving love of Christ crucified. I am most thankful for the people I have met, and I only hope that they never have to grieve about me, but that they, too, will always be certain of, and thankful for, God's mercy and forgiveness. Forgive my writing this. Don't let it grieve or upset you for a moment, but let it make you happy.

—from *Letters and Papers from Prison* 208

Additional Readings

God in the Machine

The Pauline question whether circumcision is a condition of justification seems to me in present-day terms to be whether religion is a condition of salvation. Freedom from circumcision is also freedom from religion. I often ask myself why a "Christian instinct" often draws me more to the religionless people than to the religious, by which I don't in the least mean with any evangelizing intention, but, I might almost say, "in brotherliness." While I'm often reluctant to mention God by name to religious people—because that name somehow seems to me here not to ring true, and I feel myself to be slightly dishonest. (It's particularly bad when others start to talk in religious jargon; I then dry up almost completely and feel awkward and uncomfortable—to people with no religion I can on occasion mention God by name quite calmly and as a matter of course.) Religious people speak of God when human knowledge (perhaps simply because they are too lazy to think) has come to an end, or when human resources fail—in fact it is always the *deus ex machina*★ that they bring on to the scene, either for the apparent solution of insoluble problems or as strength in human failure—always, that is to say, exploiting human weakness or human boundaries. Of necessity, that can go on only till people can by their own strength push these boundaries somewhat further out, so that God becomes as superfluous as a *deus ex machina*.

—from A Testament to Freedom 502–503

＊ *God from the Machine, a phrase Bonhoeffer uses to criticize the idea of God as a remote power who descends from on high to solve human problems, rather than the biblical image of a suffering, compassionate God.*

Follow Me

"As Jesus was walking along, he saw Levi, son of Alphaeus, sitting at the tax booth, and he said to him, 'Follow me.' And he got up and followed him" (Mark 2:14). The call goes out, and without any further ado the obedient deed of the one called follows. The disciple's answer is not a spoken confession of faith in Jesus. Instead, it is the obedient deed. How is this direct relation between call and obedience possible? It is quite offensive to natural reason. Reason is impelled to reject the abruptness of the response. It seeks something to mediate it; it seeks an explanation. No matter what, some sort of mediation has to be found, psychological or historical. Some have asked the foolish question whether the tax collector had known Jesus previously and therefore was prepared to follow his call. But the text is stubbornly silent on this point; in it, everything depends on call and deed directly facing each other. The text is not interested in psychological explanations for the faithful decisions of a person. Why not? Because there is only one good reason for the proximity of call and deed: *Jesus Christ himself*. It is he who calls. That is why the tax collector follows. This encounter gives witness to Jesus's unconditional, immediate, and inexplicable authority. Nothing precedes it, and nothing follows except the obedience of the called. Because Jesus is the Christ, he has authority to call and to demand obedience to his word. Jesus calls to discipleship, not as a teacher and a role model, but as the Christ, the Son of God.

—from *A Testament to Freedom* 90

Who Is Entitled?

At what a cost do we bring ourselves to say the name of Jesus Christ even in the presence of another Christian? Here, too, right and wrong approaches are mixed together. Who has permission to force oneself on one's neighbor? Who is entitled to corner and confront one's neighbor in order to talk about ultimate issues? It would not be a sign of great Christian insight if one were simply to say at this point that everybody has this right, indeed, this obligation. Again here the spirit of doing violence to others could insinuate itself in the worst way. In fact, others have their own right, responsibility, and even duty to defend themselves against unauthorized intrusions. Other persons have their own secrets that may not be violated without the infliction of great harm. Nor can they divulge them without destroying themselves. They are not secrets based on knowledge or emotion, but secrets of their freedom, their redemption, their being.

—from *Life Together* 103–104

Power Against Power

We have fallen into secularism, and by secularism I mean pious, Christian secularism. Not the godlessness of atheism or cultural bolshevism, but the Christian renunciation of God as the Lord of the earth. In this renunciation it becomes evident that we are indeed bound to the earth. We have to struggle with the earth to come to terms with it. There is no other way. Power stands against power. World stands against church, worldliness against religion. How could it be otherwise than that religion and church are forced into this controversy, into this struggle? So faith spruces up its weapons because the powers of the earth compel it to do so. After all, we are supposed to represent God's cause. We have to build for ourselves a strong fortress in which we dwell safe and secure with God.... Only now we want to hide not just from the enemy, the world, but even from God, from that God who destroys whoever would front for God on earth. It is not God's will that any of us, on the sheer strength of our own superabundant power, should take over for God on earth, as the strong take care of the helpless. On the contrary, God manages God's own cause and, out of God's free grace, accepts us, or does not accept us. God intends to be Lord on earth and regards all-out exuberant zeal on God's behalf as a real disservice. Herein lies our Christian secularism, that, in our very desire to see that God gets everything that is due God in the world, we actually evade God and so love the earth for its own sake, for the sake of this struggle. But we do not thereby really elude God. God always brings us back under God's own lordship.

—from *A Testament to Freedom* 90

Works Cited

Bonhoeffer, Dietrich. *Discipleship.* General Editor, Wayne Whitson Floyd Jr. Minneapolis, MN: Fortress Press, 2001.

———. *Ethics.* General Editor, Wayne Whitson Floyd Jr. Minneapolis, MN: Fortress Press, 2005.

———. *Letters and Papers from Prison.* Revised Edition, edited by Eberhard Bethge. New York: The Macmillan Company, 1967.

———. *Life Together.* General Editor, Wayne Whitson Floyd Jr. Minneapolis, MN: Fortress Press, 1996.

———. *A Testament to Freedom: The Essential Writings of Dietrich Bonhoeffer.* Edited by Geffrey B. Kelly and F. Burton Nelson. San Francisco: Harper-SanFrancisco, 1995.